Magical Arts

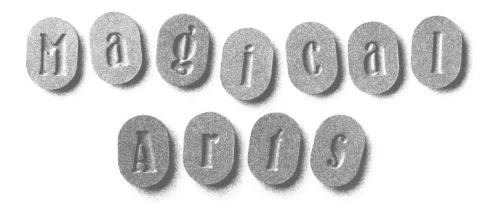

By the Editors of Time-Life Books

TIME-LIFE BOOKS, ALEXANDRIA, VIRGINIA

CONTENTS

CHAPTER 1

The Magical Animal

nited States troops invading Panama in December of 1989 made an astonishing discovery at the Fort Amador headquarters of dictator Manuel Noriega, just outside Panama City. In a secret room in Building 152, they found a collection of strange materials and artifacts—including animal entrails, a bucket of dried blood, and a ball molded from glutinous cornmeal and bound up with white string and blue ribbon. When broken open, the ball yielded a crumpled photograph of Guillermo Endara, the new president who was installed by the American forces to take control of the country from the deposed Noriega.

Another photo, this one of Ronald Reagan, was found buried beneath layers of hardened red wax, as if to transfix the former U.S. president. And a large rock covered with apparently magical symbols weighted down a piece of paper containing the names of more than a score of people Noriega counted as his enemies—including the commander of the invading American forces, Costa Rican president Oscar Arias, former U.S. secretary of state Henry Kissinger, Panama's Roman Catholic archbishop, and American ambassador Arthur Davis.

All these items, an Army expert on the occult revealed, were black-magic totems designed to weaken or immobilize the Panamanian dictator's enemies. In fact, it was learned that Noriega kept a Brazilian sorceress on his staff to work such magic on his behalf. The woman was reported to have fled Building 152—which American soldiers soon dubbed the witch house—only minutes before troops arrived, but she had left behind yet more evidence of her efforts.

Candles marked with the names of Reagan and President George Bush were discovered in a freezer, where apparently they had been placed to "freeze" the two men's actions. Other totems aimed magical effects at Senator Jesse Helms, U.N. secretary general Javier Perez de Cuellar, and ex-defense secretary Caspar Weinberger. The name of journalist Seymour Hersh, who had reported on Noriega's alleged involvement in drug trafficking, was consigned to the core of a rotting tamale.

One of the nastiest objects—and, presumably, intended by Noriega and his magician to be among the most powerful—was a stinking concoction wrapped in a red cloth. Inside was a putrid cow's tongue folded double and nailed shut with more than twenty large nails, then buried beneath white corn in a bowl that also contained eight rotten eggs. When the nails were pulled out and the tongue was gingerly unfolded, a name appeared to be written inside, but the ink had smeared to illegibility.

U.S. officials were quick to publicize the discoveries in order to promote the public perception of Manuel Noriega as a primitive and malevolent man. And indeed, the information that the ruler of a twentieth-century American nation kept a magician on his staff and resorted to the casting of spells in the conduct of affairs of state was a startling revelation to many.

But anthropologists, sociologists, and others who study trends in human social behavior could hardly have found the news surprising. For all the intellectual rationality and urbane sophistication that cloaks our modern society, belief in

magic is still widespread and deeply ingrained. The old art whose practice in centuries past struck icy fear in the hearts of those threatened by it seems never to have loosened its grip on the human imagination.

In some parts of the world, self-declared practitioners of magic thrive openly. For example, an establishment in Ibadan, Nigeria, calling itself the Divine Powers Metaphysical Center offers by mail order a Vanishing Brief Case, which, with the aid of a magic ring and secret utterance, is alleged to make its contents temporarily disappear for safekeeping. The center also sells what it calls an Invisible Cap and Cord, which supposedly enables the wearer to disappear whenever he or she feels threatened, say by thieves. (The prices depend on the costs of gathering the various magical materials needed, including rain collected before it fell to earth while a rainbow was visible, and Lightning Bullets, described as "red hot stones that are fired out of lightning.") In Panama, Noriega's interest in magic was hardly concealed; his military intelligence service ran a newspaper that carried articles about witchcraft, including a report on the arrest of an anti-Noriega sorcerer.

Even in the educated populations of industrialized nations, belief in magic flourishes, though sometimes in ways that are not instantly recognized as having any connection with magic. For instance, common superstitions, such as knocking on wood and avoiding cracks when walking along a sidewalk, demonstrate a respect for some kind of magical force, albeit one perceived only vaguely, and a willingness to perform a ritual as insurance against ill effects.

Such superstition thrives in unlikely places—Japan among them. As their business acumen and manufacturing success attest, the Japanese must be characterized as practical and rational people. Yet according to a recent poll, half of all Japanese men and women believe in unlucky years. And a large proportion exercise unusual caution on unlucky days, as spelled out in a lunar-dominated system inherited from the Chinese. Days designated *sanrinbo,* for instance, are considered particularly unfavorable for constructing buildings. Construction work on a sanrinbo day is deemed a threat to the whole neighborhood. Not long ago in the northern Japanese city of Yamagata, a man who erected pillars and a roof frame for a new house on a sanrinbo day was compelled by his neighbors to take them down. Superstition permeates the culture in other ways. Restaurant owners daily put mounds of salt outside their establishments for good fortune, and politicians begin their campaigns by painting an eye on a special lucky doll.

The Japanese, like the Chinese, ascribe names and characteristics to years, following both a twelve-year cycle of animals and a five-year cycle of classical elements (wood, fire, earth, metal, and water). Many Japanese believe that women born in years when the element fire and the animal horse coincide will be aggressive and overbearing and perhaps will even kill their husbands. According to the *New York Times,* when fire and horse coincided in the year 1966, the number of births in Japan fell by a quarter—then almost doubled the next year, as couples who had not wanted to risk giving birth to fire-and-horse daughters resumed having babies.

The Soviets, despite living in a society in which reason is supposed to prevail, have a superstitious reverence for magical healers. No less a figure than Communist party general secretary Leonid Brezhnev, who was rapidly approaching his dotage, employed a folk healer, and when the woman had worked her magic on him, he looked and acted like a restored man; indeed, to the chagrin of many, he would outlive his usefulness to the state by several years. With the advent of a more open Soviet society in the 1980s, folk healers began to use television to reach the masses.

In the United States, bizarre superstitions are plentiful, and many people abide by them—even though they may claim not to take the beliefs seriously. According to Wayland Hand, professor emeritus of folklore and Germanic languages at the University of California at Los Angeles, a surprising number of Californians preserve the habit of entering doorways with their right foot first, an inhibition that was common among Germans in the eighteenth century. Hand—who, together with a colleague, has amassed a file of almost a million such folk beliefs—does not know why Californians follow the curious right-foot-first practice. But

The "eye of Horus," named for an Egyptian sun god, peers from the bow of this Maltese ship. Early Egyptian sailors held that the amulet kept their vessel safe—a belief surviving in some Mediterranean countries.

another folklorist, Alan Dundes of the University of California, Berkeley, points out that "behavior doesn't exist without meaning. People will not practice customs unless they mean something to the psyche." When a bride tosses her bouquet over her shoulder to the female guests attending her wedding, for instance, she is performing an ancient ritual signifying that she is being deflowered and that the unmarried woman who catches it will be endowed with the necessary magic to become the next bride.

Magic exists in other forms in the United States. Thousands of fortunetellers do a thriving business in America, and while some may claim to divine the future by what they contend are nonmagical methods—such as palm reading or receiving psychic vibrations—others gaze into magic crystal balls. Sorcerers, too, find customers in the U.S. At least one voodoo doctor was practicing his brand of magic during the 1980s in a Virginia suburb just outside the nation's capital. Named Ernest Bratton but known professionally as Dr. Buzzard, he claimed to be able to cure everything from cancer to AIDS. In addition to consulting with clients personally, he peddled an instructional home video called "Voo Doo, Hoo Doo, You Do." Although he professed to know how to kill at a distance (by mixing cemetery soil with water in a hollow bullhorn, adding a gold-eyed needle, and then waiting three days before jabbing the needle into a lemon three times and repeating the intended victim's name), Dr. Buzzard said that ethics prevented him from using the technique and that he preferred curing to killing.

Outright sorcery, common superstitions, a calendrical system for determining propitious and unlucky days, folk healing, wedding customs, divination, voodoo (which many people embrace as a religion): Can all those different beliefs and activities really be lumped together under the single rubric of magic?

Some who have studied the subject say not, that the term *magic* has a more limited meaning—that it excludes anything related to religion, for instance, or that it applies only to the business of employing rituals to cast spells. Others who have pondered the question with equal seriousness have come to exactly the opposite conclusion, however, viewing magic as an even wider descriptive umbrella that encompasses in its shades of meaning yet more human activities.

The fact is that there is no general agreement as to what magic means, although plenty of definitions have been offered. One popular encyclopedia says simply that magic is "a body of traditional ritual techniques for controlling events, including the behavior of others." Similar attempts to define the term for lay purposes have specified that the rituals are designed to "bring about the intervention of a supernatural force" or that they are believed to have "a direct and automatic influence."

Sir James Frazer, a Scottish anthropologist, was one of the first modern thinkers to examine the nature and meaning of magic. In his seminal treatise *The Golden Bough*, published in 1890, Frazer said that magic involved the belief that humans, through their rituals, could directly control natural forces, whereas religion required the propitiation of divine powers who might then intervene on behalf of the human suppliants. Some writers since then have drawn an even bolder line to distinguish religion from magic—maintaining, more or less, that no ritual can be termed magic if those employing it view it as religious. Others, however, insist that it is impossible to objectively distinguish priests

from magicians and that magic is a part of virtually all religious systems. There also exists a view that prohibition of a rite by organized religion is precisely the factor that defines that practice as magic.

To some people of a New Age mindset, magic is "a stage in the quest for spiritual realities." To one sociologist versed in the jargon of his academic discipline, it is "the expropriation of religious collective representations for individual or subgroup purposes" and therefore "must have something to do with the parturition of individual monads out of the collective whole"—which to a layperson may be as obscure and impenetrable as the secret-language wording of a medieval wizard's spell. People who want to underscore their conviction that there is nothing real about magic may label it a "pretended art," a "spurious system," or a "false science."

Daniel Lawrence O'Keefe, a sociologist and writer who set out to present a general theory of magic—"a complete explanatory account of the whole thing, past and present"—related some of his difficulties in finding a way to define his subject. Magic, he said, "is first of all a universal human idea, a concept so widespread and distinct that it is almost a 'category of the human spirit,' like time, space and mass." He discovered that another sociological writer who preceded him in the territory used the word *magic* on almost every page of his book without ever saying precisely what it meant.

O'Keefe finally chose to define magic by describing a whole list of "well-known, clearly identified and unmistakable institutions" that he said are recognized throughout the world as magical in character. His broad institutional "provinces," or categories, encompassed diviners, fakirs, soothsayers and shamans, witches, black-magic sorcerers, rainmakers and ceremonial magicians, practitioners of religious magic (among whom he included exorcists of the Catholic church), astrologers, Gnostics, Hermeticists, faith healers, and a host of others, including modern cultists such as Scientologists. No doubt there are people who take exception to his choices—particularly antagonistic to his ideas are those who find their own specialties on his list. Few astrologers, for instance, would accept that their work has any connection at all with what is generally thought of as magic. But O'Keefe, who marshals convincing arguments for his categories, has at the very least clearly indicated magic's boundless reach into almost every corner of human existence.

Whatever exactly magic is, there is little doubt that it packs power, which goes a long way toward explaining why it continues to be practiced. Whether magic achieves its ends by some supernatural means as its believers contend or instead depends entirely on psychological effects for its efficacy, it seems to be able to kill, injure, cause illness, or cure. Anthropologists know well the spiritual and physical havoc that belief in sorcery can work on the susceptible. They speak of voodoo death and soul loss, conditions that cause the victims, seemingly healthy one day, to grow sick the next and eventually die, unless the spell is broken through the intervention of a shaman or witch doctor. A researcher named M. G. Marwick studied accounts of almost 200 deaths among members of central Africa's Cewa tribe and reported that only 25 percent of these were attributed to natural causes or acts of God, whereas more than double that amount were blamed

on magic—mainly, it was said, cases of sorcerers killing other members of the tribe.

Regina Dionisopoulos-Mass, a Greek-American anthropologist who spent a couple of years during the 1970s living on a small Greek island in the Aegean Sea (she called it by the pseudonym Nisi to protect its inhabitants' privacy), found that magic permeated the islanders' daily lives. Most especially, they feared the evil eye, the look that literally kills—or so they thought. They believed that no one and nothing was safe from the evil eye—neither animals, houses, bread, cheese, and plants, nor men, women, and children. Interestingly, most islanders believed that every one of them possessed the power to cast an evil-eye spell. The island dwellers considered this so because they recognized that they were all capable of one of the basest of human emotions, envy, which they regarded as the driving force behind malevolence. Thus a compliment over someone's good fortune or appearance was usually interpreted as a kind of threat in disguise, for beneath the smile and kind words could lie jealousy and the unspoken wish that harm befall the lucky person. All that was required to make such

A Hong Kong marketplace magician (right) performs an ancient folk ritual intended to stamp out an evil spirit plaguing her client. Muttering curses and wielding an old black shoe, the magician pounds a scrap of paper bearing a sketch of the tormentor.

evil incarnate was a glance of the eye.

But they also believed that some people were more likely to curse a victim with a baleful glare than others were. Dionisopoulos-Mass had direct evidence of the sway the evil eye had over the islanders. She took lodgings with an old woman called Georgia, well known for her alleged use of the evil eye. So much fear did this crone instill in the village secretary, described by the anthropologist as "a well-educated, sophisticated girl," that whenever Georgia came to the mayor's office to line up for her social-security benefit, the young woman automatically handed it to her, ahead of everyone else, to avoid arousing her ire. When the anthropologist moved out of Georgia's house, the villagers told her they had wanted to warn her about her landlady but were afraid to do so, lest they be cursed. In fact, several confessed that when they learned she was leaving Georgia's, they thought twice about inviting the researcher to come live with them, if for no other reason than that Georgia might have launched an attack against

Two stuffed figures keep watch from atop a cement wall during a May Day festival in southern Portugal. Armed only with jugs of wine, such effigies supposedly warn away a legendary bandit who once swindled the countryfolk of their silver and gold.

them for taking her in.

As Dionisopoulos-Mass gained the confidence of the islanders, she discovered the lengths to which they would go to protect themselves against the evil eye. One preventive measure was to mix flowers used at a Good Friday service with three teaspoons of salt and six teaspoons of white flour, burn them, then sew the ashes into a small bag to be carried in a pocket or attached to a piece of clothing. A mother might knit a little packet of blue thread and enclose a clove of garlic in it as a special talisman for her child. Someone else might hang a starfish or a crab's claw on the wall or rub soot from the fireplace behind an ear as protection. Even the owner of the island's single bus, who professed not to believe in the evil eye, saw to it that icons, various charms, and blue beads—blue being considered particularly effective against the eye—graced his dashboard and sunshades.

When the eye struck, the islanders resorted to a variety of cures, from the simple to the elaborate. They believed that depressions, headaches, fevers, and chills could all be caused by it and that they could alleviate these by acknowledging that envy felt by others had brought them on. More tractable cases called for complicated processes. One popular quasi-religious ceremony involved a ritual in which burning cloves helped expunge evil. The man or woman conduct-

ing the ritual first made the sign of the cross three times over the patient, then inserted a pin through one of the dried spice buds and held it over a candle flame while uttering a counter-curse: "If it is a woman who has cast the eye, then destroy her breasts; if it is a man, then crush his genitals." Again making the sign of the cross over the afflicted individual, the would-be curer now recited a simple verse imploring the Holy Trinity to remove the original curse. After the first clove burned up, a second was slipped into the flame, and then a third, and so on, until one snapped. If the sudden sound caused the patient to flinch or jump, the spell was considered broken; the evil had exited the body. But when none of the cloves snapped, the illness was deemed to be organic instead, and the sufferer was referred to a doctor for diagnosis and treatment.

Not surprisingly, magic wields enormous influence in places where people still live close to nature and are subject to its vagaries. Liberia is one such place. Out of a population of two million, 65 percent adhere to old beliefs, with their emphasis on so-called devils—actually beneficent spirits—who are thought to inhabit the bush. Families send their children to summer "bush schools" for indoctrination. There the youngsters are taught respect for magic and learn the right way to farm, fight, dance, and make use of herbal medicines.

Villagers in Devonshire, England, strain to turn the Shebbear Stone, believed to have been placed there by the devil. Local custom dictates that the stone be repositioned every year to dislodge the devil's spirit, thus averting misfortune.

The devils play an important part in village life. On occasion, someone will dress up as a devil and enter a settlement; he is readily accepted as a spirit come to solve problems, even though most of the residents know that he is, in fact, one of their own in disguise.

Despite government efforts to curtail their activities over the years, Liberian sorcerers continue to flourish. In one case more than a quarter of a century ago, lightning struck a mud hut in the settlement of Gbonwea and killed a villager. The chief called in the lightning doctor, a sorcerer who lived on the other side of a snake-infested swamp, and asked him for help. As protection against future lightning strikes, the sorcerer planted a sacred cottonwood tree beside the structure and issued three commandments: The villagers never again were to pour cooking oil on a fire, carry bunches of coconuts into the settlement, or chew the candy-coated gum sold under the brand name Chiclets. They obeyed his commands, and more than twenty-five years after the fact, no one else has been killed by lightning, so the villagers assume that the sorcerer was right to demand his bizarre discipline.

Surely one of the oddest of modern magical cures surfaced in Rhodesia, now Zimbabwe, during the 1950s and may still be used there to this day. It was devised to help people who had developed a strange new complaint—pos-

*Artists create a sand painting outside a butcher's shop in Knutsford,
near Manchester, England. Thought to bring good fortune to those who commission
them, the designs are part of an annual May celebration
commemorating an 1887 royal visit to the village.*

session by the spirit of a European. But first the so-called doctor had to examine the client to determine whether a European spirit had really invaded him. This he did by ringing a bell in the client's ear and talking to him; if the patient began to tremble and shout, he was probably in the grip of the *bindele,* or European spirit. But only after the patient had performed a wild dance on a tiny stool and then fallen over a small jar filled with chalk could the diagnosis be confirmed, although the source fails to say just why.

Doctor and client then went together to the patient's village. There the possessed one built himself a circular grass windbreak, and he remained in it for as long as it might take him to loosen the hold of the foreign spirit, anywhere from one to five months. During this period, he was expected to eat only European food—bread, tea, and other items familiar to Africans but not regularly consumed by them. Furthermore, he was to keep himself, his clothes, and his bedding immaculate.

When the patient seemed cured, he accompanied the doctor to church, to undergo a final test. There, after another display of trembling, he had to fall over a cross and keep his torso and legs from touching the ground by supporting himself on his hands. But even this accomplishment was no guarantee that he was entirely free of the bindele. His failure, for example, to rise on command would be blamed on intervening spirits; the doctor would then circle him, stamping the floor until the spirits had been driven away. Upon getting up, the patient was invited to grab one of five disks—four of them red, the other one black. If he chose a red disk, he was probably recovered, but his true condition would be determined later. In the meantime, he took a seat, joined in a sing-along with those assembled in the church, and then addressed them, reminding his audience, among other things, to keep clean, to eat well, and to take good care of their children.

This done, the patient now had to accompany the doctor into a kind of holy of holies and confide to him whether he felt truly cured. Once again he began shaking, and as the tremors rendered him all but helpless, he was expected to fall forward and grab a tree trunk with both hands for support. Only then could he be deemed fully purged of the European spirit.

Magic has the rituals and richness of age, the accretions of countless centuries to make it mystifying, compelling, and to this day, for millions of people the world over, still believable. The basic magical practice of using rituals and spells in an effort to influence real events takes several forms—none of which includes the sleight-of-hand stage version popular today, with its performers in high hats entertaining audiences by playacting the part of a magician. Serious magic includes what is called white, or good, magic, and black, or evil, magic.

These terms were sometimes used in the past to refer to the sources of magical power, which was deemed to be supernatural in origin, arising from either a beneficent spirit or a wicked one. Today the terms most often describe the intent of the magical act: White magic is used to help people, black to harm them. White and black magic can each be broken down into two additional categories: sympathetic, or imitative, magic and contagious magic. The imitative kind is based on the so-called law of similarities—the notion that a magical outcome results because of its likeness to the actions taken to achieve that outcome. The sorcerer who makes a clay or wax effigy and then sticks it with pins to indirectly afflict the person the effigy represents is practicing imitative magic. So, too, is the Oriental herbalist who prescribes ginseng for the loss of virility because the root happens to grow in the shape of a man's lower torso and must therefore be powerful medicine.

Contagious magic is founded on the law of contiguity, which holds that parts once connected continue to have an affinity for one another after separation. Thus a sorcerer might seek fingernail clippings or a lock of hair from his intended victim to use in a ritual against him. Out of fear that such personal items might fall into the wrong hands, many people in the past buried them. In Madagascar, the fear was carried to extremes: Certain servants, known as *ramanga,* had the unenviable duty of swallowing nail parings and blood lost by members of the upper class, so as to prevent these materials from being put to evil use by the masters' enemies. In fact, the nobleman who was wounded in battle or otherwise injured would have his bleeding parts licked by a faithful ramanga. Even in some cultures today, people are reluctant to be photographed, worried that in the hands of strangers their images might somehow be used to do them harm.

While noting the differences between black and white and imitative and contagious forms of magic, many scholars make yet another distinction in classifying magical beliefs. They distinguish between what they call high and low magic. The term *high magic* is reserved for actions carried out within a coherent system of magical principles. For example, the soothsayer who makes use of astrology is practicing high magic, as is the alchemist who follows the oftentimes painstaking instructions of others who went before him in the centuries-old attempt to turn commonplace metals into gold. Although the alchemist's work may be carried out in seclusion, high magic is frequently an elaborately ceremonial, communal activity designed to raise the consciousness of participants. Its rituals and practices are aimed at achieving mastery of oneself and one's environment to the point of transcending all human limitations. Such lofty undertakings are in sharp contrast to low magic, which seeks immediate worldly advantage.

Low magic is personal and mechanical: The magician performs a specific action and expects a specific result. Most of the activities surrounding voodoo in North and South America and the kahuna magic of the Hawaiian Islands are typical of low magic. They are, in the words of historian Jeffrey Russell, "employed almost technologically to attain practical ends. . . . One man fertilizes a field by slit-

*This dolmen, or table stone, located in a village in northwest France,
is said to fulfill a young woman's dreams of marriage within a year of her visiting it.
But the hopeful one must exhibit a certain skill for the dolmen to work its
magic: She must walk through the opening without touching the rocks.*

ting a hen's throat over it at midnight, another by spreading steer manure over it at dawn."

Where and when magic began is anyone's guess. Some scholars suggest that it preceded religion and that man was and, in some ways still is, a magical animal. Painting animals on cavern walls may well have given early hunters a feeling that they had some sort of control over their prey. By showing the animals as pregnant, they may also have been invoking imitative magic, in the hope that the beasts they depended on for their livelihood would reproduce abundantly and thus keep them in meat to satisfy their hunger, as well as provide leather and sinews for their clothing and tallow for their lamps. Prehistoric humans dwelling in central Europe are thought to have resorted to a special magic of their own, making figures of clay that would explode when exposed to extreme heat and then attempting to divine meaning from the shattered pieces. Interestingly, although they had discovered the secrets of baking clay in a kiln, these first potters did not, in fact, make pottery, apparently reserving their knowledge of ceramics for magical application only.

The written record offers abundant testimony to magic's importance to early civilizations. Indeed, writing itself was long seen as belonging to the province of magic, the written word having all the force of a charm. "The speech of the gods" is how Egyptians referred to their picture writing, the province of their priest-magicians; the Greeks spoke of Egyptian hieroglyphs as sacred carvings. "The word," runs one Egyptian text, "creates all things: everything that we love and hate, the totality of being. Nothing exists before it has been uttered in a clear voice." Such logic underlies incantations, whose success was dependent upon their being delivered exactly and along certain set rhythmical lines.

With words themselves magical, is it any wonder that magic could take hold of minds? To this day, shamans the world over will write magic words or spells on anything from leaves to food and will instruct their patients to eat them, thereby effecting cures. The most familiar magic word of all, abracadabra, has been traced through Aramaic, the language of Jesus Christ, to the drug-focused religious cults of Sumer and to their word, *abbatabbari,* which refers to a psychedelic mushroom.

Belief in the evil eye, too, goes well back in time, to that same Middle Eastern region where civilization began. Clay tablets from the royal library at Nineveh, the ancient capital of Assyria, tell how sorcerers could kill by merely casting a glance at their victims. The imprecation, or curse, inherent in the look "acts upon a man like an evil demon," reads one such tablet. "The screaming voice is upon him. The maleficent voice is upon him. The malicious imprecation is the cause of his disease. The maleficent imprecation strangles this man as if he were a lamb. The god in his body made the wound, the goddess gave him anxiety. The screaming voice, like that of the hyena, has overcome him and masters him."

Black magic certainly had numerous devotees in those early centuries of civilization, as various ancient texts make clear. An aggrieved Egyptian, for example, could annihilate his enemy, or so it was believed, by creating a clay figure as a stand-in for the victim and by inflicting the appropriate injury upon it.

But a clay or wax figure could also be used as white magic to restore a sick person to health, as in Assyria, where a magician would exhort the evil spirit to flee the body of the patient and enter the effigy. So, too, white magic could be used to lay the ghost of someone haunting a living person. According to the instructions for one Assyrian charm, the magician could help the victim by first writing the dead man's name on the left side of a clay figure with a stylus, then putting the effigy "into a gazelle's horn" and burying it "in the shade of a caper bush or in the shade of a thorn bush."

To keep plague at bay, the Assyrian magician followed a carefully prescribed formula: "Pull off a piece of clay from the deep, fashion a figure of his bodily form and place it on the loins of the sick man by night; at dawn make the atone-

Tibetan lay monks such as the one here, photographed with his wife in about 1930, wander the countryside with their prayer beads and other religious tools to teach the word of Buddha. Rural Tibetan religion mixes Buddhism with older magical beliefs, so monks also work spells against local gods and demons.

ment for his body, perform the incantation of Eridu, turn his face to the west, that the evil plague demon which hath seized upon him may vanish away from him.''

Another cure-all incantation covered multiple illnesses and invoked horrid creatures along the way: ''Sickness of the head, of the teeth, of the heart, heartache, / Sickness of the eye, fever, poison, / Evil spirit, evil demon, evil ghost, evil devil, evil fiend, / Hag demon, ghoul, robber sprite, / Phantom of night, night wraith, handmaiden of the phantom, / Evil pestilence, noisome fever, baneful sickness, / Pain, sorcery or any evil, / Headache, shivering, / Evil spell, witchcraft, sorcery, / Enchantment and all evil, / From the house go forth / Unto the man, the son of his god come not into, / Get thee hence!''

As such lines suggest, magicians may well have been the first doctors. An Egyptian text, in any case, makes it clear that ''he who treats the sick must be expert in magic, learned in the proper incantations and know how to make amulets to control disease.'' To become a physician-priest with magical skills, the Egyptian novice underwent rigorous training over many years. When finally a master, he set about curing. He even practiced a kind of psychotherapy, in which patients were put to sleep in a temple, possibly under the influence of a drug and, upon awaking, were invited to tell

their dreams. The priest-magician would then duly interpret the dreams, and often this was enough to relieve the patients of their symptoms. Egyptians also considered dreams a source of oracular revelation, but here, too, special rites were involved, and magical recipes were used, one of which called for laurel and olive leaves, virgin earth, wormwood seeds, and an herb called *cyncephalion,* mixed with the white of an ibis's egg.

Thanks to his powers, the magician was seen as a very special person, as one apart, often identified by certain characteristics supposedly common to his kind. He was said to have had a particularly cunning look, the evil eye. It was said, too, that the pupils of his eyes consumed the irises in which they were set, that his vision produced images back to front, that he cast no shadow. He possessed poetic or oratorical gifts and had a shrill voice. He might also display an infirmity, such as a limp. He fell easily into ecstasy and carried his onlookers along with him. Though often referred to by male gender in writings, the magician was not always a man. Excluded from membership in most religious cults, gifted women turned to the only practices available to them, namely magical ones, and became sorceresses.

Certain professions predisposed their practitioners to reputations for magic—doctor, blacksmith, barber,

This rooftop spirit trap was used to protect a Tibetan home. Empowered by shamans, such traps supposedly ensnare flying demons.

shepherd, and gravedigger. Doctors used arcane techniques and strange medicines and produced results that could be construed as miraculous; blacksmiths worked with iron and fire and forged miracles, employing secrets of their own; barbers could collect locks of hair and fingernail clippings to use against the individuals from whom these had been cut; shepherds were directly in touch with nature; gravediggers labored close to death.

Once he was seen as possessing occult powers and demonstrated that he could use them, the magician benefited from the uncritical attention people gave him. As an apparent master of forces beyond the control of ordinary individuals, he could do anything, or so it came to be believed. He could levitate, turn up in several places at once, send out his soul at will, transform himself into an animal, even seem to die and come back to life after visiting the spirit world (a common journey, incidentally, for shamans in all parts of the world).

In short, the willing suspension of disbelief that good magic engendered made everything appear possible, with magicians' astounding feats doubtlessly discussed—and distorted by word of mouth—throughout the land. Centuries ago in England, for example, who was to doubt that magicians could summon fairies? After all, the method for doing so was boldly set out in a manuscript, available to anyone who could read.

As the instructions make clear, however, "an excellent way to get a Fayrie" required an attention to detail that must have discouraged even many serious magicians: "First get a broad square chrystall or Venus glasse, in length and breadth 3 inches: then lay that glass or chrystall in the blood of a white Henne, 3 Wednesdays or 3 Fridays, then take it out and wash it with Holy Water and fumigate it. Then take 3 hazel sticks or wands of a years growth, peel them fayre and white and make them so long as you write the spirits of fayries which you call 3 times on every sticke, being made flatt on one side. Then bury them under some hill, whereas you suppose fayries haunt, the Wednesday before you call her, and the Friday following, take them up

and call her at 8, 3, and 10 of the clock which be good planets and hours, but when you call, be of cleane life and turn thy face towards the east, and when you have her, bind her to that stone or glasse."

Because credence in his powers was strong, the magician often found himself consulted in cases of thwarted love. As the records from ancient times forward suggest, he apparently had no qualms about sharing various charms and spells with his clients, but the methods of producing love charms could be complicated.

According to one set of instructions, an unrequited male lover had to fashion two clay effigies, one molded in the shape of a kneeling woman, the other in the form of a man holding a sword; he was told to position them so that the weapon was held to the female's throat. Next he was required to write the names of demons on the female doll and jab thirteen bronze needles into its legs and arms at intervals as he chanted, "I pierce the (name of the affected limb) that she may think of me." Then he was obliged to write certain words on a metal plaque, tie it to the figures with a string knotted 365 times, and bury the effigies in the grave of a person who had died while still in the bloom of youth or, barring that, of someone who had experienced a violent death. Finally, the lovesick swain was urged to deliver an incantation to the gods.

The Middle Ages shine as the period when love charms flourished, but a certain desperation lurks behind the words of the many that survive. In one appropriately breathless formula, the lover was to take three hairs from the head "and a thread spun on a Friday by a virgin, and make candles therewith of virgin wax four square, and write with the blood of a cock sparrow the name of the woman, and light the candle, whereas it may not drop upon the earth and she shall love thee." Another, supposedly more efficacious prescription exhorts the unrequited one to "take the navel string of a boy, new born, dry and powder it and give him or her to drink." A nutmeg that has been worn under the armpit for two days

Australian Aborigines perform a ritual dance in which they pretend to harvest the young from the belly of a shark totem. Through such imitative magic, the dancers seek to ensure an ample food supply for the tribe.

could work wonders as well; when it is ground and slipped into a drink, the spice had immediate effect—"she shall love thee without doubt." In an even more head-on attack, the lover is advised to place a bit of a medicinal plant known as vervain "in thy mouth, and kiss any maid saying these words, 'Pax tibi sum sensum contenerit in amore me' "— Latin for "Peace be unto you. Your feelings strain to be in love with me." Then, according to the instructions, "she shall love thee."

To help them produce magic or enhance the illusion surrounding it, magicians utilized various devices and ac-

couterments. Rods or wands remain in use to this day. One medieval account specifies that a wand should be made of "almond-tree wood, smooth and straight, of about half an ell to six feet long." Other accounts are equally specific, although no two ever seem to call for the same wood. Greek conjurers could not do without their wands or their mirrors, with which they peered into the future. Arabs had their mirrors too, made of glass or metal, from whose polished surfaces supposedly emanated the vapors in which spirits took shape. John Dee, an Elizabethan who gained a fine reputation for casting horoscopes, was reputed to possess a basalt

mirror that could give back "an image appearing in the ayre betweene you and the glass."

In time, crystal balls came into vogue and were widely used by magicians—John Dee among them—to summon spirits and foretell events. "Conjuring with the stone," as this activity was sometimes called, evolved its own rituals. One source tells what to expect: "The sign of appearance most seemeth like a veil or curtain, or some beautiful colour hanging in or about the stone or glass, as a bright cloud or other pretty kind of hyeroglyphical show, both strange and very delightful to behold." Good or bad angels might then reveal themselves in this aura. The good angels apparently were easy to identify, since they appeared as "dignified powers of light and in countenance very fair, beautiful, affable, youthful, smiling, amiable," generally with "flaxenish or gold coloured hair," and "without any of the least deformity either of hairyness in the face or body or any crooked nose or ill-shaped members." Properly addressed by the

magician, such clean-cut figures might deign to answer questions posed to them.

Invoking spirits came fraught with risk, and to protect themselves from harm, magicians drew magic circles and stood inside them, a spiritual barrier through which evil supposedly dared not penetrate. This was a tradition at least 5,000 years old. The failure to draw a circle could, as a sixteenth-century writer insisted, lead to death on the spot, "such death presenting the symptoms of one arising from epilepsy, apoplexy or strangulation." Magicians usually described the circle directly in the earth with a knife or sword. Sometimes they drew it on a piece of parchment—occasionally covering it with names, formulas, and signs written in dove blood—and carried it rolled up with them from one place to another, ready to be spread on the ground. Circles varied according to usage. Time, season, and year all had to be taken into account, as well as the types of spirits being called forth, "what star and region they govern and what functions they have."

No magicians needed the protection of circles more than the necromancers, whose practices count among the lowest and foulest, for they specialized in raising the dead and smelled of the tomb. The worst of them used corpses as their props. Dressed in clothes taken from someone who had recently died, they feasted on dog meat—dogs having been sacred to Hecate, goddess of the underworld and of sorcery—and even putrid human flesh. They were said to have injected a secret serum into those they exhumed and irradiated the bodies with beams of their own energy, whereupon the corpses allegedly rose, stumbled about, mumbled their messages from beyond the grave, and then collapsed. Other necromancers dealt with astral bodies, tracing a magic circle over a grave and stepping inside it. By a series of incantations, they strove to bring forth a phantom who would answer questions about a variety of matters, from the location of buried treasure to getting the better of enemies.

To further increase the efficacy of their magic, conjurers frequently brought into play the aromas of assorted perfumes and fumigants. "There are some perfumes or suffumigations and unctions," wrote one magician, "which make men speak in their sleep, walk, and do those things that are done by men that are awake, and often what, when awake, they cannot do or dare do. Others again make men hear horrid or delightful sounds, noises and the like." Several extant recipes leave little doubt as to why the perfumes produced such surreal effects. Hemp, *Cannabis sativa,* the basis for hashish, was a major ingredient in one fumigant, white poppy in another, black poppy in still another. The fumes of burning coriander, henbane, and pomegranate pith were enough, apparently, "to cause a man to see visions in the air and elsewhere." Interestingly enough, *cannabis* and *artemisia,* or wormwood, were reported to produce visions on the surfaces of mirrors.

Unnoticed by others who are talking nearby, a kneeling woman conceals effigies of loved ones beneath the floor tiles in this nineteenth-century Chinese watercolor. According to traditional belief, those whom the dolls represent will be magically shielded from harm.

But perfumes, fumigants, crystal balls, mirrors, and wands did not by themselves a magician make. True magicians were born to their craft or came by their skills the hard way, after years of concentrated effort. An old manuscript thought to date from the fifteenth century tells how its supposed author, a magician known as Abraham the Jew, acquired his art partly from his magician father, partly by traveling to many countries and seeking out conjurers who might teach him their secrets. But not until he arrived at the house of an Egyptian sage called Abra-melin did he find himself on "the true path" and discover "how to command and dominate evil spirits."

The account Abraham left behind sheds light on the magician's circumscribed life. "The magician's bed chamber must be near the oratory," he writes, "and the sheets and all linen changed every Sabbath eve. No dog, cat or other animal shall enter, and eating, drinking and sleeping should be in moderation and never superfluous. Especially shun drunkenness and flee public dinners."

The writer is specific about the clothes a magician should wear: "Flee all vanity. You shall have two dresses and you shall change them on the eve of each Sabbath, brushing and perfuming them always beforehand." But for the purposes of conjuring, the magician should dress up "in a shirt or tunic of linen, large and white" and a magnificent robe "of crimson or scarlet silk," which "should not be longer than just to the knees. The girdle is to be of silk, the same color as the tunic, and the beautiful crown for the head is to be a woven fillet of silk and gold."

Thus impressively attired, the conjurer set about making magic, a process that according to Abraham could take as long as seven days to complete. "If during the invocation

Simon Magus, a first-century-AD heretical magician, is borne aloft over Rome by evil spirits at the top of this Italian painting from the 1400s. Legend holds that the prayers of the apostles Peter and Paul (with halos, lower left) overpowered the demons and caused the magician to crash to the ground (foreground).

the spirits should appear with tumult and insolence, fear nothing, neither give way to anger," he advises. "Only show them the consecrated wand and if they continue to make a disturbance, smite upon the altar twice or thrice and all will be still."

Another illuminator of the magician's life, thought to have been a sixteenth-century bishop in Greece, laid down six rules by which a conjurer should be guided: "(1) the Master must have faith and doubt not in his work; (2) he must be secret and betray not the secrets of his art but to his fellows and to them of his counsel; (3) he must be strong-minded, severe and not fearful; (4) he must be clean in conscience, penitent for his sins, never willing to return to them again so far forth as God shall give him grace; (5) he must know the reigning of the planets and the times meet to work; (6) he must lack none of his instruments, and must speak all things plainly and distinctly; he must make his circle in a clean air and due time.

"Whoso observes these rules," the author noted, "by God's grace shall not miss but obtain his purpose."

Although there were always charlatans among them, many magicians did hold to a high purpose, taking themselves very seriously indeed. As a matter of fact, magicians can be divided into three categories. The sorcerer ranks lowest because of his tendency to employ black magic with intent to harm. The more high-minded magician falls into the second slot, for, having developed his faculties to a point where he can use his superphysical powers at will, he is capable of achieving physical ends denied those lacking his gifts. Moreover, he has the power to glimpse worlds beyond everyday reality. But it is the magus, or wise man, who occupies the highest category. As a supermagician, he employs his knowledge of the arcane to penetrate to the very meaning of life.

Magus, magician, and sorcerer, all three subscribed to the ancient belief that whatever is below is like that which is above, and whatever is above is like that which is below, often condensed into the phrase, "As above, so below." This dictum was the first of several tenets of magic engraved, it was said, on an emerald tablet and wrested from the stiffened hands of a mummy by no less a historical figure than Alexander the Great.

ere was expressed the notion that the universe is a single interconnected organism, a great unity, and that anything that affects one of its parts affects all of them. In this grand scheme, humans existed as microcosms of the macrocosm, or universe, and because the two shared an affinity, the magician, with his special powers, could draw upon the connection to achieve his ends. The idea persists today; the rainmaker shaking water on the parched earth from a soaked branch is creating a mini-rainstorm, a microcosm for the macrocosm of the sky to imitate.

Astrology, long one of the tools of the magician, sprang naturally from the concept of a direct linkage between humans and planets. Palm reading made a similar leap, even going so far as to regard each finger and its joints as being under the rule of a particular planet and each palm wrinkle as having universal meaning. Divination, a favorite of the ancients, saw omens of the future in the organs of animals, the movements of birds, the arrival of deformed babies, the patterns of oil dropped on water, and a host of other phenomena.

Magicians reasoned that if a man or woman was nothing less than a mirror of the cosmos, then it must be possible somehow to fathom and understand existence itself. One magician even went so far as to proclaim that "no one has such power but he who has cohabited with the elements, vanquished nature, mounted higher than the heavens, elevating himself above the angels to the archetype itself, with whom he then becomes co-operator and can do all things."

Pythagoras, the sixth-century-BC Greek, was as much a magician as he was a mathematician, and in his pursuit of an answer to the mystery of life, he developed an avid following. He founded a secret society, whose members had to go through a difficult initiation and then adhere to strict rules that demanded of them silence, abstinence, vegetarianism, and deep self-analysis.

Among some of the odder restraints that dominated their lives were prohibitions that forbade eating beans or putting on the left shoe before the right. Pythagoras enjoyed a reputation for being a great healer who employed music and incantations to effect his cures. Using only magic words, he summoned an eagle from the heavens, tamed a bear, drove away venomous snakes, and persuaded an ox to stop eating beans—or so it was said. However apocryphal such stories may be, Pythagoras was a solid thinker, and he proposed that numbers were the basis of all understanding—that all relationships in nature could be expressed numerically.

Pythagoras would be only one of the many who attempted to uncover the secret laws governing the universe. For some of these seekers, life's great purpose was to come to grips with the wonderful unity that bound humankind, earth, and the universe together, and magic was the way to accomplish this. Nothing, it seemed, was without meaning to the one who could read the signs expressing this linkage. Among the Jews, the belief that the one true way to approach God was through knowledge grew into what is known as the Cabala, a system or collection of occult thoughts and speculations added to and passed on orally by Jewish mystics over the centuries.

The Cabala posited a ladder by which the enlightened might climb toward the deity. Ten points of light, the so-called *sefirot* that emanated from God himself, linked by twenty-two paths, the number of letters in the Hebrew alphabet, awaited seekers after the truth. But the climb was an arduous one, with each point fiercely defended by guardian angels who had to be overcome before the next point could be gained. The names for God were believed to be many, with the individual letters considered so potent that they could bring about miracles. Eventually, cabalistic writings and signs themselves came to be seen as having magical potential and were incorporated into amulets. The Cabalists had the ability to put out fires, call forth spirits, and

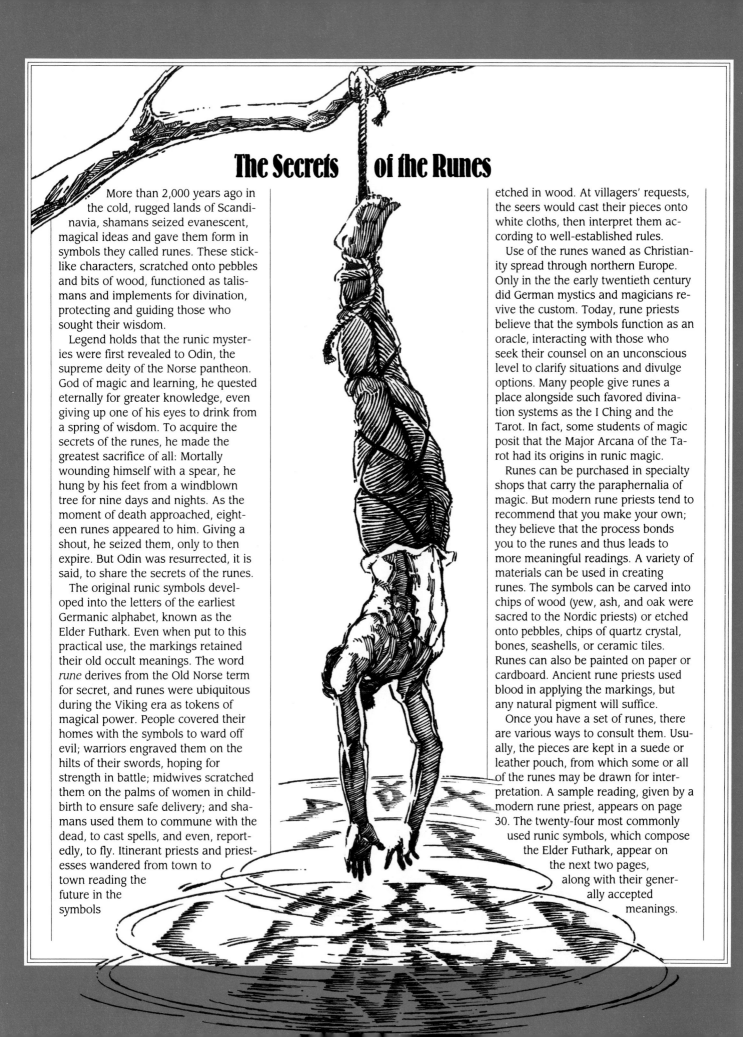

The Secrets of the Runes

More than 2,000 years ago in the cold, rugged lands of Scandinavia, shamans seized evanescent, magical ideas and gave them form in symbols they called runes. These stick-like characters, scratched onto pebbles and bits of wood, functioned as talismans and implements for divination, protecting and guiding those who sought their wisdom.

Legend holds that the runic mysteries were first revealed to Odin, the supreme deity of the Norse pantheon. God of magic and learning, he quested eternally for greater knowledge, even giving up one of his eyes to drink from a spring of wisdom. To acquire the secrets of the runes, he made the greatest sacrifice of all: Mortally wounding himself with a spear, he hung by his feet from a windblown tree for nine days and nights. As the moment of death approached, eighteen runes appeared to him. Giving a shout, he seized them, only to then expire. But Odin was resurrected, it is said, to share the secrets of the runes.

The original runic symbols developed into the letters of the earliest Germanic alphabet, known as the Elder Futhark. Even when put to this practical use, the markings retained their old occult meanings. The word *rune* derives from the Old Norse term for secret, and runes were ubiquitous during the Viking era as tokens of magical power. People covered their homes with the symbols to ward off evil; warriors engraved them on the hilts of their swords, hoping for strength in battle; midwives scratched them on the palms of women in childbirth to ensure safe delivery; and shamans used them to commune with the dead, to cast spells, and even, reportedly, to fly. Itinerant priests and priestesses wandered from town to town reading the future in the symbols

etched in wood. At villagers' requests, the seers would cast their pieces onto white cloths, then interpret them according to well-established rules.

Use of the runes waned as Christianity spread through northern Europe. Only in the the early twentieth century did German mystics and magicians revive the custom. Today, rune priests believe that the symbols function as an oracle, interacting with those who seek their counsel on an unconscious level to clarify situations and divulge options. Many people give runes a place alongside such favored divination systems as the I Ching and the Tarot. In fact, some students of magic posit that the Major Arcana of the Tarot had its origins in runic magic.

Runes can be purchased in specialty shops that carry the paraphernalia of magic. But modern rune priests tend to recommend that you make your own; they believe that the process bonds you to the runes and thus leads to more meaningful readings. A variety of materials can be used in creating runes. The symbols can be carved into chips of wood (yew, ash, and oak were sacred to the Nordic priests) or etched onto pebbles, chips of quartz crystal, bones, seashells, or ceramic tiles. Runes can also be painted on paper or cardboard. Ancient rune priests used blood in applying the markings, but any natural pigment will suffice.

Once you have a set of runes, there are various ways to consult them. Usually, the pieces are kept in a suede or leather pouch, from which some or all of the runes may be drawn for interpretation. A sample reading, given by a modern rune priest, appears on page 30. The twenty-four most commonly used runic symbols, which compose the Elder Futhark, appear on the next two pages, along with their generally accepted meanings.

Fehu

Fehu, the first rune, is a powerful symbol of bounty. Depicting the horns of cattle or oxen, the rune originally represented material wealth in the form of livestock. It may also have signified the plow and fertility of the fields. Today, Fehu indicates prosperity of any kind, material or spiritual. As a rune of fertility, it may also suggest an actual or symbolic birth.

Uruz

An ideogram for the aurochs —a large, long-horned wild ox that is now extinct—Uruz represents the strength and freedom of that animal and symbolizes creative power, sexual energy, and physical health. When Uruz appears in a reading, it counsels the inquirer to think about harnessing his or her energies in the interest of personal growth.

Thurisaz

Thurisaz represents a thorn and bears painful messages, warning of cruelty, deceit, or a rude awakening to a previously hidden truth. Associated with Thor, god of thunder and lightning, this rune symbolizes cathartic destruction. But while it predicts unhappiness to come, Thurisaz also indicates that the way is clear for new beginnings.

Ansuz

Most mystical of all the symbols in the Elder Futhark, Ansuz represents the mouth of the wise god Odin, discoverer of the runes. It marks the link between Odin and modern rune magicians, signifying truth, verbal expression, and clarification. Inquirers who draw Ansuz should take heed: An important message may be forthcoming.

Raidho

Raidho is the rune of travel. It originally represented a chariot, signifying the path of the initiate as he or she climbed to higher levels of magical knowledge and experience. Today, Raidho indicates a physical or spiritual journey or quest. Drawing this rune suggests that the inquirer is moving toward the realization of a goal.

Kenaz

Fiery passions may be in store when the inquirer selects Kenaz, the flame of a torch. Associated with Freya, the Norse goddess of love, this rune represents the positive aspects of human passion and sexual love. It also indicates creativity and generation on a physical level. As the torch, Kenaz offers illumination, lighting the way through darkness.

Gebo

Gebo, meaning gift, traditionally pertained to the gifts of the gods, one of which was rune magic. Modern interpretations of this rune include gifts of any sort, even selfless actions. Gebo's intersecting lines also indicate union or partnership, possibly of a sexual or magical nature.

Wunjo

Joy is predicted when the rune Wunjo is drawn. It suggests happiness and harmony among people and delight in one's accomplishments. A symbol of restoration, Wunjo also promises clarification of things previously unclear and the opening of areas formerly blocked. The inquirer who draws Wunjo may expect changes for the better.

Hagalaz

In opposition to Wunjo is Hagalaz, or hail. In its icy storm, the inquirer may suffer setbacks and hardship. However, change and liberation are part of its message: If current upheavals are handled wisely, they will lead to a brighter future. Symbolizing the Nordic concept of a cosmic ice egg filled with magical power, Hagalaz promises joy and warmth, but only after a thaw.

Naudhiz

This symbol represents human struggle in the face of adversity. Naudhiz, meaning need, indicates an overwhelming compulsion to achieve something. The inquirer who draws the rune is invited to examine his or her motivations and to separate true needs from desires. Trust fate, Naudhiz counsels, for it will ultimately guide you to what you need.

Isa

Isa, or ice, represents life in stasis, where change and growth are absent. The symbol, a single line, suggests the individual ego, coldly separate from others; it also denotes the sustaining force during times of stress. Thus the ice rune urges the inquirer to consider areas of his or her life that may be frozen and suggests reliance on inner strength in struggling free.

Jera

Jera means "the year," and its symmetrical symbol suggests the seasons' cycle. This rune offers the inquirer a waiting period, allowing time in which growth may occur naturally. Cyclic development, natural fruition, and the passage of time are watchwords for Jera.

Iwaz

Sacred because it symbolizes the yew tree from which Odin hung to capture the runes, Iwaz signals the traits inherent in that evergreen. A hardy, long-lived conifer, the yew protects against evil, according to Scandinavian legend. Drawing Iwaz assures the inquirer continued growth even in the face of adversity.

Perthro

Perthro depicts a dice cup, contributing an element of chance to the runes. It relates to the Old Norse concept of ørlög, the layers of past action—either individual or cosmic—that shape the present. The inquirer is challenged to accept the fact that in certain areas fate controls all.

Elhaz

The symbol for Elhaz is a stylized hand with the fingers splayed, a universal symbol of protection. The inquirer who draws Elhaz will be blessed during tribulation and will face temptation without succumbing. This rune also forms a bridge between human consciousness and the divine, alerting the inquirer to prepare for enlightenment.

Sowilo

Sowilo, the sun, counters the freeze of the ice rune Isa. It predicts challenging periods of spiritual growth, embodying the inquirer's most difficult goal but also promising a path leading toward that objective. Sowilo foretells transformations that, like the sun's heat, can be extremely intense.

Tiwaz

Rune of the Norse god Tyr, Tiwaz stands for his qualities of bravery, truth, and justice. According to myth, Tyr once sacrificed his own hand to the jaws of a wolf in order to save another god from destruction. Drawing this rune signifies that sacrifice and courage may now be required in the name of justice.

Berkano

A stylized depiction of a woman's breasts, Berkano, or the birch goddess, is the runic symbol for the concept of mother earth. It relates to the cycles of life—birth, coming of age, marriage, and death—and promises the blessings of peace and fertility. Its association with the birch tree pertains to the inquirer's physical and spiritual environment.

Ehwo

Ehwo, the two horses, symbolizes the means of reaching a physical or spiritual destination. Composed of two elements, the symbol speaks of the trust and loyalty shared by horse and rider and predicts the harmonious cooperation of two forces pursuing a single goal. The peaceful union of two people in an emotional relationship may also be foretold by Ehwo.

Mannaz

Mannaz is the runic symbol for the self. One expert describes it as the mystery of the divine embodied in the individual. The power of human intelligence, rationality, and memory are highlighted here. Although it generally relates to a single person, Mannaz may also address a couple that functions as a single unit.

Laguz

A rune of initiation, Laguz, the lake, signifies water. It was originally associated with the pagan baptism of newborns. The rune also suggests emotion, intuition, and dreams, and the inquirer who draws it should pay special attention to the messages of the unconscious mind.

Ingwaz

Representing an old Germanic god who consorted with the earth mother, Ingwaz signifies fertility and gestation. It warns that adequate time—a gestation period—must be allowed in order for difficult tasks to be completed. At the end of such a period, however, the inquirer will emerge from this chrysalis of toil to experience deliverance.

Dagaz

Dagaz is the day: a message of awakening, clarity, and transformation. It promises a short waiting period for the completion of a process. Dagaz has been described as the break of dawn, a mystical moment in which all opposites—darkness and light, pleasure and pain, life and death—can be expected to meld. The inquirer may await a revelation when it is drawn.

Othalo

Othalo means ancestral property or homeland and relates alternatively to the inquirer's family or to his or her spiritual or professional heritage. Othalo encourages the inquirer to examine the ways in which his or her roots inform the present; the rune also recommends evaluation of the beliefs and habits learned from one's elders.

Wyrd

Wyrd, the blank rune, is not part of the Elder Futhark, but it is often included in purchased rune sets. Similar in meaning to Perthro, Wyrd stands for fate and mystery.

When drawn in a reading, it represents an unattainable quantity, reminding the inquirer that some knowledge is beyond reach and must remain forever a mystery.

Consulting the Runic Oracle

The manner in which runes are cast depends in part on the needs of the inquirer. For example, someone seeking quick insights into his or her current situation might choose to interpret a single rune selected from the set at random. On the other hand, someone who needs a more detailed assessment might toss the entire set and interpret all the runes that land face up.

Other methods of casting runes include reading a specific number of pieces, usually three or five, and reading runes that are arranged in traditional patterns. Shown on this page is a five-rune pattern, or spread, known as Thor's hammer. Each position in the spread holds particular significance, and the runes are read in a set order (indicated here by the numbers). Thor's hammer is used to address a single topic, selected in advance by the inquirer. In this example, a woman requested help in clarifying her professional goals. The reading was conducted by Gaffer MacCluiunn, a rune priest who works in Washington, D.C.

MacCluiunn began by asking the woman to select five runes at random. He explained that her unconscious mind would interact with the runes, allowing her to select the symbols that held the most personal meaning. He arranged the pieces in the order in which she drew them.

The first position in Thor's hammer always relates to the inquirer's general situation. The woman drew Perthro, the dice cup, which suggested that answers to questions about her career might wind up being left to chance. MacCluiunn saw this as a plea to the inquirer to take control of her life. The

2. Elhaz

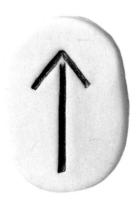

3. Tiwaz

rune counseled that the act of choosing was extremely important.

The second rune position foretells how the inquirer's present situation will play out if nothing is changed. The woman selected Elhaz, which foreshadowed protection and stability in her present career.

Position three, here occupied by the rune Tiwaz, predicts the outcome of a situation if changes are made. Tiwaz warned that great courage and honesty would be required if the inquirer chose to change her situation. It recommended that she be truthful with herself about her goals and that she pursue them bravely.

The fourth position tells the inquirer which element in a situation is most open to change. The woman drew Kenaz, the torch, which indicated that she might need to alter her passions and desires in the interest of achieving her objectives. The rune urged that she look deeply in her heart to determine exactly what she wanted. The advice of others would not be helpful; she would have to rely on her instincts.

Finally, the constant elements in an inquirer's situation are revealed by the fifth rune. In this reading, Iwaz turned up in that position. As the yew tree, Iwaz symbolized hardiness and stability. It assured the woman that, like the evergreen, she would thrive regardless of her professional fortunes.

4. Kenaz

1. Perthro

5. Iwaz

banish diseases, it was said, through the amazing power of words and numbers.

During the Middle Ages, cabalistic thinking and its attendant magic became an important influence on the development of high, ceremonial magic in Christian Europe. Swept up by it, one of the foremost magicians of the Renaissance era, the sixteenth-century German Cornelius Heinrich Agrippa, wrote, "Immovable numbers and characters breathe forth the harmony of Godhead, being consecrated by divine assistance therefore, the creatures above fear them, those below tremble at them."

As the notion of a universal spirit permeating all existence took hold in many minds, new energy was brought to an old quest, alchemy. From earliest times forward, people had sought the means to turn base metals into gold and silver. In Egypt, the priest-magicians controlled metallurgy as a secret craft; a great body of knowledge grew up around the subject, and many of the methods and formulas eventually came to be recorded in obtuse alchemical books. When some would-be alchemists in ancient Rome availed themselves of this know-how and began palming off as precious metals alloys that passed for gold and silver, the emperor Diocletian decreed that the old books be burned to protect the economy.

The works of the Greek philosopher Aristotle, saved from oblivion by Arab scholars and widely disseminated throughout Europe, became an influential force in alchemical studies and experiments. Aristotle believed that the earth had been shaped from prime, or first, matter, something that could be neither seen nor touched but that had taken on initial form from the four basic elements—earth, air, fire, and water. Moreover, because he saw these elements as sharing certain physical qualities (hot and cold, dry and moist), he reasoned that substances like metals could be changed by altering the proportions of the qualities they had in common. To his way of thinking, lead and gold were not as unlike as people supposed; the trick would be to alter their components in such a way that lead would change to gold.

Inspired by Aristotle and other voices from the past, alchemist-magicians during the Middle Ages set about to do nothing less than tap into the prime matter, to go to the heart of the universe, the fifth element, as it were, and create the so-called philosophers' stone. This was envisioned as an object so quintessential and marvelous that it could be used not only to transmute common metals into precious ones but also to cure illnesses and extend life. It was described variously as being yellow, dark red, and the color of poppies and of carbuncles. As though to reconcile the conflicting descriptions, one writer stipulated that "this stone unites within itself all the colours. It is white, red, yellow, sky-blue and green."

In Germany, Cornelius Heinrich Agrippa embraced the belief that humans were miniature replicas of the universe, of God himself, and that all things were permeated by the Universal Spirit. He saw this spirit as descending to the earth in starlight and contended that various metals, gems, and herbs thus came under the influence of particular stars or planets. He recommended that charms that could change "sickness into health or health into sickness" be fashioned from materials that had been star-blessed. Agrippa believed it possible to extract the spirit from a valuable metal and transfer it to a less valuable one, therefore rendering the second priceless, but years of fruitless experimentation had brought only bitter frustration.

"There is no greater madness," Agrippa wrote sourly of those obsessives who would give up everything in the pursuit of alchemy, "than to believe in the fixed volatile or that the fixed volatile can be made—so that the smells of coal, sulphur, dung, poison and piss are to them a greater pleasure than the taste of honey—till their farms, goods and patrimonies are wasted, and converted into ashes and smoke; when they expect the rewards of their labours, births of gold, youth and immortality, after all their time and expenses; at length old, ragged, famished, and with the use of quicksilver, paralytic; only rich in misery, and so miserable that they will sell their souls for three far-things; so that the metamorpho-sis which they could have pro-duced in the metals, they cause to happen in themselves—for in-stead of being alchemists, they are cacochymists; instead of be-ing doctors, beggars; instead of unguentaries, victuallers; a laughing stock to the people."

However, once he had ex-pressed his disappointments, Agrippa could not help but ad-mit that "many excellent inven-tions owe their orgin" to alche-my, including "azure, cinnabar, minium, purple, that which is called musical gold, and other colors." (Cinnabar and minium are both red mineral com-pounds.) He conceded as well that "we derive the knowledge of brass and mixed metals, sol-ders, tests and precipitants" from alchemy. Thanks to the al-chemists, in other words, chem-istry had taken a great leap for-ward. Indeed, the discovery of sulfuric ether, hydrochloric acid, zinc, phosphorous, benzoic ac-id, caustic potash, and dozens of other substances can be attrib-uted to them.

Occasionally an alchemist would claim to have actually come up with the much-sought-after philosophers' stone and, in the face of the doubters, pro-duce convincing evidence that

A crumpled newspaper bursts into flame, appar-ently ignited by the electric touch of an Indone-sian healer dubbed Dynamo Jack by Britons investigating his powers. Dynamo Jack claims that, with enough meditation and practice, any-one can harness the energy to perform such spectacular, seemingly magical feats.

he had indeed happened on a process verging on the miracu-lous. Johann Friedrich Helvetius, a seventeenth-century Dutch-man, was one of those who had no truck with alchemy. Yet when Helvetius received a tiny piece of the philosophers' stone ("a substance resembling glass or pale sulphur") from an honest stranger, as he called him, and wrapped it in yellow wax and then dropped it into molten lead, the lead turned to gold—or something that looked like gold. Not trusting his eyes, Helvetius took the metal to a goldsmith, "who declared at once that it was the finest gold he had ever seen, and offered to pay fifty florins an ounce for it." Helve-tius was sufficiently impressed to have prayed afterward that the angels watch over the alche-mist, whom he now regarded "as a source of blessing to Christendom" for his ability to create wealth.

Similar tales of disbelief being transformed into credence abound in the lore of alchemy. One story relates that at Germa-ny's University of Helmstedt in 1621, a Professor Martini went to great pains to tell his students why transmutation could not possibly work—but had to eat crow when he became con-vinced that an alchemist had converted lead to gold before his very eyes. A couple of decades later, according to another tale, a reputed philosophers' stone was brought to the court of Holy Roman Emperor Ferdinand III and tried out in the presence of the director of mines. Trusting no one but himself to conduct the demonstration, Ferdinand took the stone and, using only a smidgen of it, converted two and a half pounds of mercury to gold—or so the story goes. As a precaution against fraud, he supposedly repeated the experiment, with the same results. To commemorate the event, the emperor had a medal coined, on which was inscribed "Divine Metamorphosis Caused in Prague, 15 January 1648, Witnessed by His Holy Imperial Majesty Ferdinand III."

A more detailed account of a skeptic becoming convinced of alchemical reality involves Wolfgang Dienheim, a seventeenth-century professor from Freiburg, Germany, and the Scottish alchemist Alexander Seton. The two met on a journey from Zurich to Basle, during which Dienheim attacked the alchemical art and Seton just as vehemently defended it, promising to put on a demonstration that would convince Dienheim once they reached Basle. In that city, the two men met with Jacob Zwinger, a well-known scientist and physician, and arranged for his help in setting up the transmutation.

Dienheim and Zwinger both later wrote detailed reports of what they did and witnessed. To reassure Dienheim and Zwinger of his probity, Seton picked up his materials from sources Zwinger recommended—lead from a mineworker, a crucible from a goldsmith, and sulfur from an apothecary—while in the company of the two men. Moreover, they said, he took care not to personally touch any of the equipment or materials. The other two researchers set up the crucible, built the fire, and put in the lead and sulfur under his direction.

After letting the mix melt in the crucible, Seton told Dienheim: "Drop this little paper into the molten lead, but well in the middle as nothing should fall into the fire." As he did so, Dienheim noticed that the paper held a yellow powder. After a quarter of an hour had passed, Seton stirred the mixture with iron rods. Before Dienheim's and Zwinger's eyes the concoction took on the luster of gold. "Now," asked Seton triumphantly, "where are your pedantries?" To allay any further doubts, he cut the hardened gold in pieces and gave them to the men. "You disbelievers will probably laugh at this true story," Dienheim wrote afterward. "But I am alive and ever ready to testify to what I have seen. And Zwinger is also alive. He will not remain mute, but be a witness to what I confirm."

Is magic real? To many in the past, the question would not even have occurred. Nor would it occur in some societies today where belief still runs deep. But what is one to think when rational twentieth-century men and women, as skeptical of magic as Dienheim and the emperor Ferdinand III were in their day, come around in their thinking and admit to the possibility that there might be something to magic after all. Ernesto de Martino, an Italian professor of the history of religions with a special interest in anthropology, ethnology, and parapsychology, puts himself squarely on the side of the believers. He says magic is real, if for no other reason than that it works. But he also says it draws upon paranormal phenomena that have yet to be adequately explained. De Martino claims magic is largely ignored by researchers in the field—that is, by scientists who have lived among the various primitive peoples for whom magic is commonplace—because they have already dismissed it as being implausible, as nonsense, and thus have eliminated it as a possibility.

Two Englishmen, the brothers Lawrence and Lorne Blair, the first an anthropologist, the second a filmmaker, approached magic with a more open mind when they traveled throughout Indonesia several years ago. "It was the scent of living mysticism that had first drawn us to Indonesia," wrote Lawrence in *Ring of Fire,* an account of the brothers' adventures on some of the nearly 14,000 islands that make up the country. They sought out sages, mystics, and healers and found them in plenty, if Lawrence's narrative is to be believed, as well as "ember-eaters and hypno-tists, fakirs and charlatans." Magic took the form of "a trance of every kind—even, in the Gorong Islands, a sinister form of mass possession, in which an entire village was victimized by a giant money-eating serpent, cannily articulated by prancing shamans."

By far the most remarkable individual, however, was an Indonesian-born Chinese whom the Blairs met on Java and on whom they bestowed the name Dr. Dynamo Jack. This enigmatic individual was a healer who carried out his cures in a strange and marvelous way—by self-generated electrical shock, hence the brothers' name for him.

While reluctant to be photographed, Dynamo Jack was always quite willing to demonstrate his powers to the Blairs. In the brothers' first encounter with him, he asked Lawrence to place a hand on his bare stomach, just below the navel, and told him to keep it there. "I found myself having to lean against him with all my strength," recalls Lawrence, "and still my hand was being pushed away from his stomach by what felt like a dry but irresistibly strong jet of water." Then Lawrence grasped hold of Dynamo Jack's outstretched hand. "He inhaled and released such a powerful jolt through my arm that I howled and snatched it away." But Jack was not yet finished with the Englishman. The healer asked an assistant to bring out a stool and some chopsticks and challenged Lawrence to drive one through the wooden seat. Try as he might, Lawrence could not do so, failing to leave even a dent in the wood. Jack then grabbed a chopstick and with one quick movement effortlessly drove it through the seat. "It's very simple," he announced. "Just a matter of practice."

Dynamo Jack explained the source of his energy. "Like an electric eel, we all have Yin-Yang polarity," he said, pointing downward, Lawrence writes, "from his navel with one finger, and upward from between his legs with another." Jack referred to his poles as "my positive and my negative," noting that "one comes up from the earth, the other comes down from the sky. It's just a matter of learning to harness and project them outside the body. I've been prac-ticing this for seventeen years now, meditating every day."

The brothers took to following Dynamo Jack on his rounds, watching him cure his patients with his electrical powers. When the Blairs' mother, "a rigorous judge," came to visit, they invited Dynamo Jack to her room on the ninth floor of a Jakarta hotel and asked him to show her what he could do. "Very difficult to work with these energies when so far from the ground," he apologized. But then he "crushed our newspaper into a ball, held it in his left hand, pointed at it with his right, and ignited it into a blossom of flame." Lawrence noted "a sudden strong smell of ozone in the room," as the witnesses to the feat scrambled "to get all the burning, floating pieces into the metal wastebasket before they singed the carpet."

The Blairs had long been eager to photograph Dynamo Jack demonstrating his powers, but he had steadfastly refused their requests. "I am not interested in tricks," he would say. "I am a healer. If Western people see this on film, they will assume I am a market conjurer." Thus, the brothers were more than surprised when on a return trip to Indonesia, they found Jack a willing subject. As the filming began, "he explained that he was depleted from the healing he had done that day, but went on to ignite our newspapers, push chopsticks through stools, and 'electrocute' our bodies and those of our skeptical film crew." When Lorne, who was experiencing problems with an infected eye, first had his temples touched as part of a cure, "he began jerking around so violently" that Lawrence had to ask him "not to ham it up so much, or no one would believe anything on camera. I shut up, though, when Dynamo Jack touched my hand, and jolted me into remembering what it had been like the first time.

"When I asked him why he had suddenly consented to being filmed, he replied that, now his students were starting to get the hang of it, it seemed time to show more of this to the world.

" 'Even if most people do think it's simply a trick,' he said, 'some will recognize that we all have these powers, sleeping within us.' "

The Power of Talismans

In hopes of swaying Fortune, medieval Europeans like the couple in the 1449 Flemish painting above often visited masters of the magical arts to commission engraved, coin-shaped objects called talismans. Such charms, carried in a pouch, were thought to attract favorable influences. The two talismans shown here, for example, invoke the powers of the planet Venus and were probably designed to induce love.

Most Western talismans reflect the tradition of the Cabala, the mystical body of ancient Hebrew wisdom that holds that all things in creation are related to one another through a network of correspondences. By incorporating special symbols, inscriptions, or materials associated with a planetary or spiritual power—Venus, in the charms above—a talisman is supposedly imbued with like power, which can then be wielded by the charm's owner. Some elements used in talismanic magic appear on these pages; details about the creation of personal talismans are on pages 40 and 41.

Charms That Harness a Planet's Force

The seven heavenly bodies regarded by the ancients as planets are thought to influence a particular area of human life. Thus each talisman is designed to express the power of either Saturn, Jupiter, Mars, Venus, Mercury, the Sun, or the Moon. To strengthen the bond between talisman and planetary force, charm makers use mystical symbols and pay heed to such traditional beliefs as the metal, color, and day of the week said to correspond to the planet.

Each planet is also associated with one of seven archangels and with a benevolent spirit, called the Intelligence. On a talisman, these names supposedly invoke divine assistance. Every planet has a so-called magic square, or *kamea,* made up of rows of numbers. The sum of any row—vertical, horizontal, or diagonal—equals the same number, one sacred to that planet. Charm makers assign numerical values to letters, usually the Hebrew

alphabet, to plot out names on the kameas with connecting lines whose diagrammatic forms are called sigils. (Note below the sigil for Saturn, on the kamea whose numbers its lines connect.) To the right of the planet's kamea below is the sigil for the planet, then the sigil for the Intelligence.

Some talismans feature other non-planetary symbols and magical elements said to harness unearthly energies. They appear on pages 38 and 39.

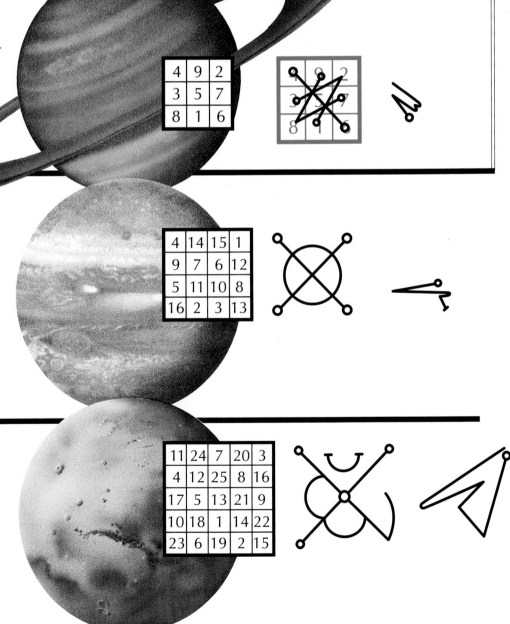

Saturn

Saturn is said to influence business and politics, property deals, agriculture, mining, archaeology, and the building trades. It also corresponds to morality and the shouldering of responsibilities. Some say that Saturn talismans protect women in childbirth and prevent death by poison or conspiracy.

METAL *Lead*
COLOR *Black*
DAY OF THE WEEK *Saturday*
ARCHANGEL *Zaphiel*
INTELLIGENCE *Agiel*

4	9	2
3	5	7
8	1	6

Jupiter

Power, legal and commercial transactions, financial speculation and the acquisition of wealth, marriage and remarriage, education, religion, and philosophy are all associated with Jupiter. Additionally, Jupiter talismans may be used to protect travelers, foster friendships, preserve health, banish anxiety, and establish sympathy in others.

METAL *Tin*
COLOR *Blue*
DAY OF THE WEEK *Thursday*
ARCHANGEL *Zadkiel*
INTELLIGENCE *Yophiel*

4	14	15	1
9	7	6	12
5	11	10	8
16	2	3	13

Mars

The planet Mars is thought to influence police matters, war, sports, engineering, machinery, and male sexuality. It is also said to favor surgical undertakings as well as development of physical strength and courage. A Mars talisman is believed not only to protect its owner from enemies but even to help overthrow them.

METAL *Iron*
COLOR *Red*
DAY OF THE WEEK *Tuesday*
ARCHANGEL *Camael*
INTELLIGENCE *Graphiel*

11	24	7	20	3
4	12	25	8	16
17	5	13	21	9
10	18	1	14	22
23	6	19	2	15

The Sun

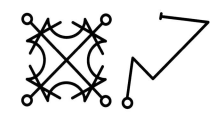

The Sun is associated with nobility, leadership, career advancement, large commercial ventures or business undertakings, the judiciary, banking, fatherhood, and the performing arts. It is thought to promote self-confidence, health, virility, friendship, and powers of divination and to help dissolve hostile feelings.

METAL *Gold*
COLOR *Gold*
DAY OF THE WEEK *Sunday*
ARCHANGEL *Raphael*
INTELLIGENCE *Nakhiel*

6	32	3	34	35	1
7	11	27	28	8	30
19	14	16	15	23	24
18	20	22	21	17	13
25	29	10	9	26	12
36	5	33	4	2	31

Venus

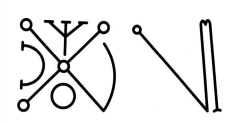

Under the dominion of Venus fall matters of love, courtship, and marriage. This planet is also said to influence personal and business partnerships, the negotiation of contracts or settlements, the visual arts, leisure pursuits, female sexuality, and an individual's income. Its powers allegedly protect women from cancer and all from poison.

METAL *Copper*
COLOR *Green*
DAY OF THE WEEK *Friday*
ARCHANGEL *Aniel*
INTELLIGENCE *Hagiel*

22	47	16	41	10	35	4
5	23	45	17	42	11	29
30	6	24	49	18	36	12
13	31	7	25	43	19	37
38	14	32	1	26	44	20
21	39	8	33	2	27	45
46	15	40	9	34	3	28

Mercury

Talismanic magic says Mercury governs road, rail, and air travel, commerce, healing, the media, mathematics, science, and industry. Intelligence and eloquence are also attributed to the planet, as is the power of prophecy. Some claim that a Mercury talisman will aid deceitful undertakings, such as theft.

METAL *Mercury or zinc*
COLOR *Purple*
DAY OF THE WEEK *Wednesday*
ARCHANGEL *Michael*
INTELLIGENCE *Tiriel*

8	58	59	5	4	62	63	1
49	15	14	52	53	11	10	56
41	23	22	44	45	19	18	48
32	34	35	29	28	38	39	25
40	26	27	37	36	30	31	33
17	47	46	20	21	43	42	24
9	55	54	12	13	51	50	16
64	2	3	61	60	6	7	59

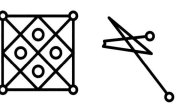

The Moon

The Moon is said to correspond to all matters pertaining to water, including navigation, voyages, and maritime trade. This heavenly body is also thought to influence motherhood, fertility, children, the home, and other domestic issues. Those wishing to start new ventures or enhance their psychic powers may benefit from a lunar charm.

METAL *Silver*
COLOR *Silver*
DAY OF THE WEEK *Monday*
ARCHANGEL *Gabriel*
INTELLIGENCE *Malka Betharshesim*

37	78	29	70	21	62	13	54	5
6	38	79	30	71	22	63	14	46
47	7	39	80	31	72	23	55	15
16	48	8	40	81	32	64	24	56
57	17	49	9	41	73	33	65	25
26	58	18	50	1	42	74	34	66
67	27	59	10	51	2	43	75	35
36	68	19	60	11	52	3	44	76
77	28	69	20	61	12	53	4	45

Potent Symbols and Mystical Words

Formed by two interlocking triangles, the hexagram is associated with divine order and destiny. The symbol is believed to protect against fire, deadly weapons, and the perils of travel. The hexagram is best known for its use as the Jewish Star of David—in Hebrew, Magen David, or David's Shield.

The circle, one of the most powerful of all occult symbols, represents infinity, eternity, unity, the universe, the Sun, heaven, and perfection. Inscribed on most talismans, the circle serves to contain and concentrate the magical energy necessary to summon the appropriate powers or spirits.

An embodiment of the number three, the triangle relates to body, soul, and spirit; father, mother, and child; past, present, and future; wisdom, love, and truth. In Christian doctrine, the triangle represents the Holy Trinity of the Father, Son, and Holy Ghost.

ABRACADABRA
ABRACADABR
ABRACADAB
ABRACADA
ABRACAD
ABRACA
ABRAC
ABRA
ABR
AB
A

The magic word abracadabra, whose meaning remains mysterious, is sometimes the sole element of a talisman. It is thought to bring good luck as well as to effect healing. As part of what is called a diminishing spell, the word is written repeatedly, with each successive line dropping a letter to form an inverted triangle. The charm will supposedly diminish the wearer's illness at the same rate the word abracadabra dwindles.

S	A	T	O	R
A	R	E	P	O
T	E	N	E	T
O	P	E	R	A
R	O	T	A	S

Magic squares in which letters spell out the same words vertically and horizontally are often found on talismans. Best known is the enigmatic SATOR square (above), which dates to Roman times and is still used for protective magic. The ROLOR talisman (right), created by a fifteenth-century magician, purportedly enables the wearer to fly like a crow.

AGLA

The letters at left are an acronym for Ate Gebir Leilam Adonai, Hebrew for "Thou art mighty forever, O Lord." They invoke God's name and allegedly infuse a charm with divine power. In the Middle Ages, AGLA was used to ward off fever.

The pentagram symbolizes the human body, with its five points corresponding to the head, arms, and legs. With one point upward, the shape is also associated with God and is used to invoke the powers of goodness. When inverted, with its single point downward, it represents the forces of evil.

Perhaps the oldest talismanic symbol in the world, the cross is an emblem of prosperity, life, and divine protection from evil. Some believe it represents the four quarters of heaven and can thus invoke heavenly powers. Christians associate it with eternal life and resurrection.

Since long before its association with Nazi Germany, the swastika has been a worldwide symbol of longevity, good luck, and happiness, and followers of magic use it to attract those qualities. The ancient symbol also represents the four winds, the four seasons, and the four directions of the compass.

When read from right to left in accordance with the Hebrew language, each horizontal row in the letter square below—a detail from a medieval talisman—spells one of the four great names of God. The sacred words, which supposedly invoke divine assistance, are commonly found on talismans made according to cabalistic tradition. A guide to the Hebrew alphabet appears to the right of the charm.

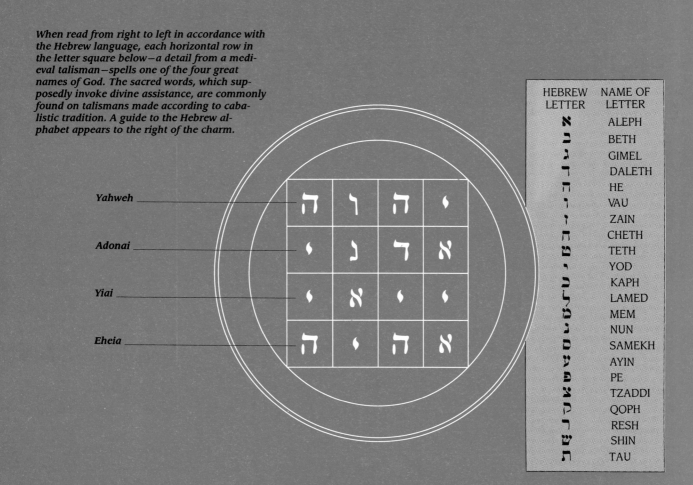

Yahweh

Adonai

Yiai

Eheia

HEBREW LETTER	NAME OF LETTER
א	ALEPH
ב	BETH
ג	GIMEL
ד	DALETH
ה	HE
ו	VAU
ז	ZAIN
ח	CHETH
ט	TETH
י	YOD
כ	KAPH
ל	LAMED
מ	MEM
נ	NUN
ס	SAMEKH
ע	AYIN
פ	PE
צ	TZADDI
ק	QOPH
ר	RESH
ש	SHIN
ת	TAU

A Talisman with a Personal Touch

Anyone creating a personal talisman such as the contemporary example presented here must first decide what purpose the charm is to serve—to help further one's career, for instance, or enhance athletic abilities. Once the goal is fixed, the planet thought to in-fluence that sphere of life can be de-termined *(pages 36 and 37)* and the un-dertaking can begin.

The charm maker starts by engrav-ing a circle on a section of metal cor-responding to the planet—or simply by drawing a circle on a piece of appro-priately colored paper or parchment. The next step is to inscribe—on either side or both—any of the symbols asso-ciated with the targeted planet. The talisman creator can then add any shapes, words, names, or verses that exemplify the forces the charm is in-

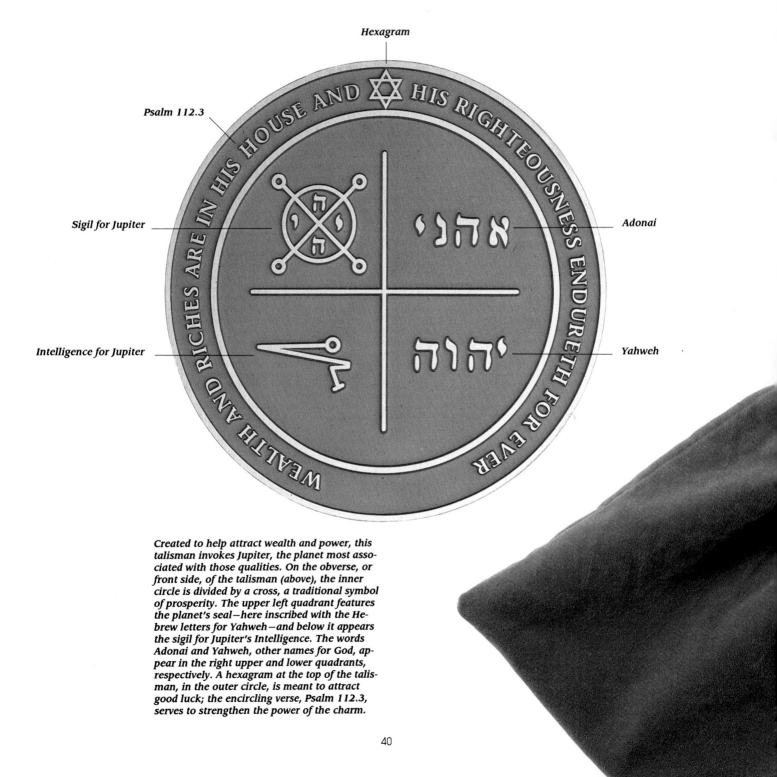

Hexagram

Psalm 112.3

Sigil for Jupiter

Intelligence for Jupiter

Adonai

Yahweh

Created to help attract wealth and power, this talisman invokes Jupiter, the planet most asso-ciated with those qualities. On the obverse, or front side, of the talisman (above), the inner circle is divided by a cross, a traditional symbol of prosperity. The upper left quadrant features the planet's seal—here inscribed with the He-brew letters for Yahweh—and below it appears the sigil for Jupiter's Intelligence. The words Adonai and Yahweh, other names for God, ap-pear in the right upper and lower quadrants, respectively. A hexagram at the top of the talis-man, in the outer circle, is meant to attract good luck; the encircling verse, Psalm 112.3, serves to strengthen the power of the charm.

tended to invoke. Although Hebrew is the traditional talismanic script, any language may be used.

Once the talisman is complete, adepts say, it must be purified to remove any unwanted energies. Metal talismans may be passed through fire, although bathing them in clear water is said to be just as effective. Paper talismans may be held up to the wind or passed over smoking incense. Next, according to tradition, the talisman must be consecrated to charge it with magical powers. This ceremony should take place on the day of the week related to the planet, believers say, but otherwise may be tailored to personal taste. It can be performed nude or clothed, indoors or outdoors, by candlelight or moonlight, say adepts—as long as the consecrators do something out of the ordinary and speak their intent aloud.

After consecration, the charm is supposedly ready to work its magic. Talismans are usually stored or worn about the neck in a silk pouch, the color of which should relate to the planet invoked.

Sum of any row in kamea

Kamea for Jupiter

Personal symbol

Astrological glyph for Jupiter

Total sum of kamea

Here, on the reverse of the talisman, is the kamea, or magic square, of Jupiter. Above and below the kamea are the planet's two sacred numbers—one the sum of each row in the square, the other the sum of all the numbers. Flanking the kamea are Jupiter's astrological glyph (right) and two stalks of wheat, chosen by the talisman maker as a personal symbol of wealth and fertility. Authorities in magical practice say that a talisman need not be decorated on both sides in order to be effective; the strength of the owner's intent is said to matter more than the composition of the charm.

CHAPTER 2

High Ceremony, Lofty Aims

he room was windowless and all but dark, a single flickering candle providing the only light. On one otherwise bare stone wall was the painted image of a coiled snake, spewing venom from its mouth. To the sides of the chamber, a scattering of men waited in the ghostly shadows cast by the candles. At the center, deep in thought and lost to the world around him, the magus sat staring into space. At his feet were his wand, his dagger, and the body of a dead snake. He was a small, portly man with waxy black hair swept away from his pallid forehead. After several minutes of pin-drop silence, he snapped to attention and proclaimed repeatedly in Latin, "Qui agnoscit mortem, cognoscit artem"—meaning roughly, "He who has knowledge of death knows the art of dominating it."

The magus's voice was oddly vivacious as he proceeded to question his audience about the rite they had come to witness. That night in 1783, the initiated brethren of the Masonic temple would determine whether one of their members should be elevated to master magician. To do so, they would consult the spirit of a wise man from another time. Their magus was Count Allessandro di Cagliostro, a controversial personage whose reputation ran the gamut from saint to devil incarnate. He would direct the Masons in conjuring the spirit, but he would need one more assistant.

Presently, a girl no more than twelve years old was led into the circle of magicians. Clad in a white linen robe, she was taken by the magus onto his knee. Steadying her with a hand placed on top of her head, he tapped the child lightly three times with the flat of his sword, once on each shoulder and once on the brow. He addressed her as Colombe—the French word for dove—and proceeded to describe the nature of the evening's work, ordering her to commend herself to the Eternal One.

"I pray Thee," said the child with prompting from the magus, "to forgive my past errors and implore Thee, because of my innocence and of the power with which the Grand Cophta, high priest of the great Temple, endows me, to help me know the truth and grant me the grace which I implore of Thy goodness and Thy mercy." The voice of the magus was gentle and reassuring, but all the while in his heart he was offering the child as a sacrifice. He mentally dispatched her to the realm of the dead, whence she might carry back knowledge not accessible to the living. The ritual required as much.

Cagliostro then sent Colombe into an adjoining chamber and locked the doors behind her, so that she could be heard but not seen. On a table at the center of that room, a glass ball and a carafe of water shimmered in the light of two candles. Outside, the magus described four circles with the tip of his sword, careful to move the blade only from left to right. As he completed each circle, he performed an insufflation—that is, he blew air from his mouth onto the Mason being tested. And at each circle he pronounced a word of invocation: ''Helion,'' at the first two; ''Melion,'' at the third; and ''Tetragrammaton,'' at the last. When these steps were completed, Cagliostro was ready to address the world of the spirits.

''My child,'' he called to Colombe, ''repeat with me the words I am about to speak: Moses, in the name of the Eternal One I order you to appear before me, without causing me any terror, taking upon yourself an agreeable form and answering me truthfully.'' Colombe dutifully echoed the man's words.

The occasion was just one of scores of such magical ceremonies staged by Cagliostro in Masonic temples throughout Europe during the latter half of the eighteenth century. Whether the Old Testament patriarch actually materialized could only be conjectured, even by those believers who were present. The wily magus always structured his ceremonies in such a way that only the child medium was expected to set eyes on the spirit apparitions. But contemporary accounts of his rituals would have us believe that Moses and other equally hallowed figures did respond to Cagliostro's call. And the Masons who did the reporting were the sorts of people who would normally be considered credible witnesses. They were bankers, lawyers, and government officials—the cream of the intelligentsia in many cities. They were not, on the other hand, really witnesses at all, since only the children would have made contact with the spirit world.

Cagliostro came to be celebrated as the most powerful magician of his day. He built his reputation as a magical healer and a formidable diviner of the future. His pronouncements touched on everything from affairs of state to the winning numbers in upcoming lotteries. But the fame of this magus was at least partially attributable to the richness and complexity of the rituals he enacted to liven his public performances. These were not his creations, however. Like other masters of ceremonial magic, he attributed his skills to secrets inherited from an ancient body of occult knowledge. In a sense, he was an artist with an audience to please; and he undoubtedly saw that it

In the eighteenth century, wandering magician Allessandro di Cagliostro found steady employment as a healer and diviner in Masonic lodges all across Europe. In the end, he was condemned as a fraud by the Inquisition and died in a dungeon.

was to his advantage to make use of recognizable magical forms. His rituals, though personalized, were filled with the cherished symbols and procedures of magic, elements sure to strike a responsive chord in any group of observers.

Cagliostro's reputation—a mixed bag even during his lifetime—has not fared well beneath the glare of historical inquiry. Most modern investigators regard him as a charlatan and a scoundrel. And indeed he left enemies scattered across England, France, Germany, Austria, Russia, and Poland who were convinced that he was an impostor and who testified to his misdeeds. Whatever Cagliostro's faults, however, he was indisputably well versed in a wide variety of magical traditions. His ceremonies incorporated elements of medieval alchemy, Masonic ritual, the Jewish Cabala, Roman magic, the Greek Eleusinian mystery cults, and perhaps most important, the Egyptian Cult of the Dead. This last tradition, in turn, is thought to have drawn upon still-older Mesopotamian magical practices. While most histori-

ans condemn Cagliostro as a rogue, a few at least acknowledge that he may, for a time, have been sincerely interested in unlocking the secrets of magic.

The type of magic Cagliostro performed is called high, or greater, magic because it is grounded in elaborate metaphysical and theological doctrines and it involves ceremonies comparable to religious rituals. The study and practice of high magic is kept alive today by small but—at least for the moment—growing numbers of people who identify with the wizards, druids, shamans, and witches of the past. Today's ritual magicians are as likely to be women as men. As in the past, their magic is collective in purpose. The magician seeks to serve the interests of his or her audience or, at a minimum, to raise their thoughts to a higher plane. In contrast to the lesser, or low, forms of magic—the more mundane arts of potions, charms, hexes, and everyday cures—high magic requires its performers to embrace something akin to a religious calling. The magicians are expected to be steeped in the philosophies and spiritual beliefs underlying their rituals.

Present-day magicians, even those who style themselves high priests or high priestesses, differ from their predecessors in that they wield little influence outside their own ranks. In past centuries, the masters of ceremonial magic often became prominent and exercised substantial power by commanding the attention of rich and poor alike. The magus filled a role not unlike that of a cleric in that he looked beyond the normal limits of human understanding and contemplated aspects of existence that defied comprehension in everyday terms. The occult, the world of the unknown, was his self-assigned domain.

But for all the rich and varied cultural influences that have made up the tradition of high magic, it has, as often as not, been the bailiwick of swindlers and frauds. There were exceptions. A mysterious first-century Greek magician and philosopher called Apollonius of Tyana, for one, seems to have spent his entire life roaming the earth in search of occult knowledge that would enable him to aid humankind. Certain fifteenth- and sixteenth-century alchemists were also upstanding in their search for spiritual perfection. But Cagliostro was far from alone in living by his wits as a ritual magician. History is littered with sorcerers, well known and obscure, who wielded their knowledge of the old magic purely to their own advantage.

John Dee, who earned a respected place in the court of Elizabeth I on the strength of his skills as an astronomer and mathematician, was high minded in his efforts to explore the occult during his younger days. But later in life he linked up with a charlatan named Edward Kelley and ruined his reputation. Perhaps the most celebrated high priest, Johann Faust of Germany, was in truth a relatively insignificant figure during his lifetime. His reputation spread when the English dramatist Christopher Marlowe made him the subject of a play. After the play appeared, the legend grew that Faust had secured his magical powers by bargaining with the devil. Even the high magicians of this century have tended to be more infamous than admired. The self-styled Great Beast, Aleister Crowley, ultimately betrayed his calling by using high magic to satisfy his ego and his lust for women *(page 65)*.

Rituals, incantations, and practices like those adopted by Cagliostro and the other high priests of magic pose unique problems for the scholars who study them. Not the least of the difficulties is that most of the traditions from which the procedures were drawn were themselves essentially secretive. Many of the practices of ritual magic were passed along orally from one generation to the next. Others, though preserved in writing, were described in cryptic language supposedly intended to render the magic inaccessible to scoffers and to civil authorities who might be made uneasy by the implicit threat it held. Magicians hoping to produce one old Egyptian curse were instructed to utter: "Osirisesengenbarpharanges. Erikisepheararaacharaephthisikera. Rikiseph-theararacharaephthisike. Base. Lord angels, as this frog vanishes away and dries up, so may the body of . . ."—and here the sorcerer would name the victim. Another popular ruse was to frustrate the reader with free-flowing mixtures of Hebrew, Latin, and Greek. Some writings were also intentionally erroneous so as to throw antagonistic investigators off the path of understanding.

In the view of some scholars, however, the paucity of authoritative texts on these customs has little to do with fear of prosecution or the desire for exclusivity. Most of the literature claiming to document ceremonial magic is altogether bogus, fraudulent compilations of alleged magical practices passed off by their authors as works of antiquity. The tome *The Secret of Secrets,* subtitled *The True Grimoire,* was written in the 1600s by a magician called Toscraec. But its author claimed that the work was based on a manuscript ignored for centuries because it was written in an unknown language. Only the help of an angel, he said, allowed him to translate the text. Other spurious writings were attributed to famous figures in history or scripture, such as Abraham and King Solomon, and their authorship came to be accepted as fact. The *Grimoire of Honorius* is unusual in that it claims to be the work of Pope Honorius III and is prefaced by a supposedly official papal bull.

British historian E. M. Butler, who spent a lifetime sifting through the literature of magic, blamed the shortcomings of most printed texts on the rigid requirements set out for such works by the magicians themselves. To be duplicable, sorcerers believed, an account of a particular act of magic had to be written down by the magician using consecrated pen and paper. As a result, source books on magic

Dolls Imbued with Lively Spirits

For more than 2,000 years, Pueblo peoples have made their home in the majestic but arid mesa country of Arizona and New Mexico. Theirs is a difficult world, and the quest for supernatural aid figures importantly in their lives. Every earthly thing, the Indians assume, has its spiritual counterpart.

Of all the Pueblo tribes, the Hopi developed the most elaborate system for petitioning the spirits, whom they call kachinas. The Hopi think of the kachinas as their ancestors or as messengers sent by the lesser gods. Some, like the cloud spirits, are more visible than others. In order to communicate with the hidden kachinas, the Indians give them material reality in the form of human impersonators and dolls.

During the kachina season, from December through July, a cycle of dances and ceremonies takes place and hundreds of kachinas appear in the Hopi villages. The kachinas are asked to promote the harvest and bring rains and to initiate, discipline, and instruct the children. Tradition holds that a man dancing the part of a spirit actually becomes the spirit—so communication can be direct.

The Hopi believe that only males can impersonate the supernaturals, but they carve replicas of their kachinas, like the ones shown here, for females of all ages to use in ceremonies. The dolls, or *tihus*, are shaped from the roots of cottonwood trees and embellished with symbols, rattles, shells, and feathers. Once they are completed, the dolls are treated not as playthings but as sacred effigies.

This doll represents the ogre Nataska, one of the demon spirits who might visit disobedient children during the February Powamuya, or Bean Dance. With his frightening countenance, horns, headdress, belt, and blood-stained ripsaw, he demands that youngsters pay for their bad behavior with food. In this way, it is hoped, they will learn self-discipline, obedience, and humility.

Cloud spirits such as Salako Taka, represented by this tihu, are thought to bring rain and thus hold special importance for the people of a dry land. Since spirits are believed to reside in the mountains and reveal themselves as clouds, the costumes of many dolls echo a cloud motif. The lofty headdress and eagle-feather skirt of this kachina give it an appropriately airy appearance.

This harvester kachina, outfitted like a corn dancer, embodies the guardian spirit of the corn crop, around which all Hopi life revolves. The Hopi religion dictates the elements that decorate a particular kachina—in this case, a bandoleer of facsimiles of corn kernels, a rattle, fresh twigs, and pheasant and macaw feathers.

were laborious to produce and thus rare and valuable. A certain traffic arose in bogus texts created by nonmagicians purely for profit. Some were based on authentic works but were less than scrupulously accurate copies.

Given the nature of ceremonial magic, slipshod descriptions of ritual procedures represented a serious stumbling block. The arts of the magus have always been characterized by an intense fastidiousness and a requirement for precision. Before conjuring a particular spirit, for instance, a magus might prepare by meditating for twenty-one days on the life and writings of the dead person being invoked. All the while, the conjurer would abstain from eating meat, and he would observe a strict fast for the final seven days. Magicians were expected to conform to tradition in the most minute details of their procedures as well. One ritual, for example, finds the magus anointing a lead plate with the blood of a bat, then sewing it up in the stomach of a frog with a bronze needle and thread blessed by the god Anubis. Later, he will suspend the frog from a reed, using string made from the tail hairs of a black ox.

During a ritual, if the wrong word was used in a spell—or even if a word was misspoken—the whole ceremony might be nullified. Even worse, according to some accounts, slight mistakes in procedures sometimes resulted in dangerous, even fatal, repercussions for the participants.

An incident in Pasadena, California, would seem to demonstrate that the element of danger continues even to this day. In June of 1952, a rocket-propulsion expert named John Whiteside (Jack) Parsons from the California Institute of Technology was blown to bits in his garage laboratory. Newspaper accounts of the death attributed the accident to the scientist's carelessness while handling cordite and fulminate of mercury. Fellow scientists, familiar with Parsons and his work, insisted that it was absurd to suggest that a chemist of his stature could have erred in mixing such basic compounds. A friend later revealed that Parsons, a follower of Great Beast Crowley, had been attempting to reconstruct a rather bizarre alchemical process dating from the Middle Ages. He was hoping to create what is called a homunculus—a tiny artificial man that, once called into being, would assist its creator by means of magical powers.

Mixing danger and esoteric lore, chicanery and high-minded mysticism, ritual magic always was filled with contradictions. Even in its heyday, it encompassed both benevolent and malicious magic and treated the two as if they were essentially the same. For the magus, the distinction between black and white magic seems to have rested not in the magician's intent but in the source of the supernatural powers needed to accomplish his objectives. Black magic, in this framework, was the conjuring of diabolic forces, while white magic entailed the invocation of religious spirits. Both were centered on doctrines of unseen, intelligent powers, with whom it was possible to communicate.

Throughout history, ritual magic and religion have coexisted in close proximity. The nineteenth-century French historian Jules Garinet argued that most of the diabolism that occurred in late medieval France was the work of idle monks who donned disguises at night to invert the Christian rites they observed during the day. Usually they parodied the Catholic mass in devil-worship ceremonies called black sabbaths. In support of this, Garinet observed that in most criminal trials of sorcerers and sorceresses the scene of the sabbath was shown to be near a monastery.

Perhaps a more reliable explanation was that people often turned to ritual magic when the ministrations of orthodox religion seemed to fail. The mental disorder that began afflicting Charles VI of France in 1393 offers a case in point. In his mid-twenties, Charles's memory began to falter, until he was soon unable to recognize his family. He swung from periods of overpowering rage, when he tore at his clothes and smashed furniture, to spells of apparent paranoid delusion, in which he became convinced that he was made of glass.

Many in Charles's court attributed his troubles to acts of sorcery, and when the king's devout prayers for respite failed to bring him relief, his advisers commissioned a variety of churchmen and magicians to effect a magical cure.

Two Augustinian monks were brought in from Guienne to attempt an exorcism. They lived at the expense of the court for several months, providing assurances that Satan would divulge to them the identity of the magician casting the spell on the king. Eventually they blamed the powerful duke of Orléans, a blunder that got them beheaded.

With the king incapacitated, the duke of Burgundy, Philip the Bold, assumed de facto control of the realm. At his suggestion, Charles submitted to treatment by a pair of supernaturalists named Poncet de Solier and Jean Flandrin. In July of 1403, the two would-be healers set up a base of operations in a thick woods near the gates of the duke's seat of power in Dijon. They erected a large iron circle of enormous weight that was held off the ground by five-foot-high iron columns. To the circle they attached twelve iron chains. Then they asked that a dozen townsfolk come forward to be shackled to the curious structure. One of the chosen was the bailiff of Dijon, who reluctantly agreed to participate but went on record as believing that the entire scheme was absurd. He declared that if he managed to survive the experience and was proven correct in his view of the magicians, he would roast the impostors.

Once the twelve volunteers were chained in place, Solier and Flandrin began a series of magical incantations. Matters continued in this fashion until the patience of Philip the Bold was expended, and by then it was clear to all involved that the ritual would have no beneficial effect upon King Charles. True to his word, the bailiff, once unchained, arrested the sorcerers and set about arranging for their immolation. As they were being led to the stake, they were asked why their ritual had not succeeded. The best they could offer by way of explanation was that all twelve participants had made the sign of the cross as they entered the circle and, by so doing, had destroyed the spell. More than likely it was pure coincidence, but the deaths of Solier and Flandrin were long remembered in Dijon, because shortly after they were burned, a storm ravaged the surrounding countryside, wasting the wheat fields and vineyards.

The ministrations of adventurers like Solier and Flan-

drin would seem an odd substitute for the prayers that were Charles's first response to his incipient madness. But the history of ritual magic is filled with such incongruities. One of the more curious contradictions ran deep in the nature of high magic: On the one hand, the magus set himself apart as a spiritual leader and was widely esteemed as such. On the other hand, the procedures he carried out were frequently lowly and degrading.

The conceit underlying high magic was that the magus pursued his art at the very point of juncture between the realms of the living and the dead. In theory at least, the energies at his disposal were titanic, because he could alternatively enlist and coerce the cooperation of supernatural beings. That being so, it may seem surprising that his rituals revolved around such base elements—roots, excrement, animal parts, ashes, vivid sexual symbology, and the language of subjugation and degradation. But the magician's rituals were constructed to embody extremes: He was trying to bridge the gap between the living and the dead, and to do so he appealed to the powers of good and evil. In a passage of the *Grimoire of Honorius,* the magus was told to slaughter a lamb and tear out a black rooster's eye to summon up the devil, while at the same time praying aloud to God.

The drama enacted in every ritual in one way or another sought to bring about an exchange between two poles—the natural and the supernatural. The magus used ritual to effect an exchange between himself (or his medium) and the spiritual realm. Once this end was achieved, so the theory went, he could use the power gained in the exchange for whatever earthly purpose he desired.

Despite the many influences that gave shape to the European tradition of high magic, all of its practices seemed to have certain common elements. In broadest terms, they were the spell, the ritual, and the magician. The spell was always verbal, and the words had to be uttered precisely, even down to the intonations. This held especially true for proper names. In all societies, names are believed to hold mystical, conjuring powers. Today, corporations spend fortunes to discover new names for themselves that will lodge securely in the public mind. But among magicians, names were more likely to be matters of the utmost secrecy.

Count Allessandro di Cagliostro (an assumed name, to be sure) took great pains to keep his real name a secret. Scholars agree that Cagliostro was, in fact, Giuseppe Balsamo, a minor Sicilian artist. When asked outright on one occasion, he replied, "Who am I? I don't know!"

In Cagliostro's case, the adopted name was perfectly in character with his penchant for deception. He also went by the title marquis di Pellegrini at one point in his career. But it was tradition among the great magicians of Europe to change their names in pursuit of spiritual regeneration. The practice was based on a custom of the Knights Templars, a religious order established in twelfth-century Jerusalem to protect European pilgrims to the Holy Land. The Templars are said to have derived the practice from an injunction of Saint John: "You must be born again." Paracelsus, the great medieval alchemist, was born in Einsiedeln, Switzerland, with an eminently discardable name, Theophrastus Bombast von Hohenheim. In contrast, the English physician and Rosicrucian Robert Fludd took as his name the odd-sounding title Robertus de Fluctibus.

In ancient Egypt, when a pharaoh was ousted, one of the first things his successor did was to obliterate all evidence of the previous ruler's name. If the name was gone, so was the pharaoh—or so the logic went. Things were not always quite so simple, however. It was common among the Egyptians to take several names, some for public use and some for private circulation. And a person's real name was kept a closely guarded secret. The rationale behind this confusing arrangement was to thwart potential enemies who might invoke one's name in a spell. A common accolade used to describe a person of great power among the Egyptians was "Even his mother does not know his name."

The Egyptians, in fact, left the first detailed descriptions of the practice of ritual magic. They believed that they were ruled by gods who walked among them in the persons of their pharaohs. Upon death, the pharaohs were thought to move on to an existence that befitted their nature as deities. The earliest magical ceremonies in Egypt, dating from the third century BC, were contrived to assist the pharaohs in making this transformation. Recorded with painstaking accuracy in the repository that we now call *Book of the Dead*, the rites have been extraordinarily influential in shaping the rituals and spells of subsequent civilizations. At first, the Egyptian practices were exclusively magical, but as they came to be addressed more directly to the gods, they took on a tone that made them seem more like religion.

Egypt's great magical guide was not originally a single book. Several hundred rolls of papyrus found at various locations throughout the country were assembled to compose our current record. The papyri contained roughly similar materials—spells, incantations, prayers, hymns, and rituals—but in many different versions. There were hymns that invoked the names of all the gods and in various ways demonstrated a thoroughgoing knowledge of the afterworld; the songs were presumed to prove one's identity as a deity and thus guarantee admittance into the supernatural realm. Other passages offered protection from all and sundry dangers, ranging from dismemberment to total extinction, or "second death."

Creating these documents was evidently a major industry for the Egyptians. Scribes would produce a scroll for any paying customer, detailing the procedures for safeguarding bodies in the tomb, making the journey to the netherworld, propitiating the gods, and taking up a new existence in the world of the dead. For many centuries, the contents of the papyri were known in Europe principally through the interpretations of Greek scholars and magicians, who were greatly intrigued by the beliefs and customs of Egypt. Not until the 1890s were Western scholars able to formally consolidate or reconstitute the many different accounts into a single text, which, because of its subject matter, was given the name *Book of the Dead.* Some Egyptologists worry, however, that many of the fragments included in the work are actually imperfect or partial renderings of writings now permanently lost.

In the early stages of their civilization, the Egyptians had a peculiar relationship with their gods. They believed, first of all, that everything in nature was inhabited by spirits. Mountains, rivers, animals, and objects came to be associated with particular deities. The spirits that were hostile to humankind were identified with certain animals and reptiles. Apep, for example, was the serpent-devil of mist, darkness, storm, and night; he was regarded with terror and yet was believed to have weaknesses of his own. The curious part of the Egyptian religious view was that it held that the gods were fallible: They could be bribed, cajoled, threatened, and flattered just as mortals could be. In fact, if one were in possession of the proper spell, a god could even be controlled. Thus, the Egyptians placed a high value on any system of magic that would assist mortals in coping with the gods. The papyri summarized in *Book of the Dead* constituted precisely that.

The book, therefore, describes in great detail what—and who—the deceased would encounter during the passage to the next world. It explains what would be asked and answers each question. It makes clear the importance

A papyrus scroll from the Egyptian Book of the Dead depicts a ceremony called the Opening of the Mouth, in which priests endeavor to restore speech and use of the senses to the corpse of a powerful man. The priest supporting the mummy wears a mask of the embalmer god Anubis. The chief celebrant (far left) is wearing vestments of leopard skin as he blesses the room with incense and carries a vessel for ritual libations. Egyptian ceremonies were widely imitated by other magicians.

*A variety of poisonous or otherwise dangerous animals
decorate this Egyptian magic wand dating from around 2000 BC.
Fashioned from animal bone, it was intended to ward off
the evil powers of the creatures pictured on it.*

of correct pronunciation and intonation when using the names of the deities. The Egyptians believed there was a secret rhythm that Thoth, the god of magic and—not coincidentally—the inventor of language, had taught to the earliest magicians. Knowledge of this rhythm and mastery of the spirits' true names were the keys to controlling the gods. To the Egyptians' delight, the highest powers of the universe were subject to domination by mortals through the power of words.

In keeping with this, the scribes recorded the story of a man called Ani whose scroll instructed him to say these words when he reached the river where the ferryman waited to take him to the world of the dead: "Oh, thou guardian of the mysterious boat, I hasten, I hasten, I hasten. I come to see my father Osiris." When the boatman replied, "Tell me my name," Ani carefully intoned: "Darkness is thy name."

Many aspects of Egyptian ritual magic survived in later cultures. One of the most lasting contributions was the myth of Isis and Osiris, which has been recycled even in present-day rituals. The origin of this myth is unknown, but it is similar in theme to stories that arose in many other early Bronze Age cultures. Some scholars have attributed the story to the Hebrews. One writer suggested that Isis was derived from a Mayan goddess, Queen Moo, who fled Central America in prehistoric times and resettled in northern Africa.

Isis was usually depicted with a vulture headdress and a papyrus scepter in her hand. Two horns above the headdress hold a solar disk between them. A Roman scholar, Apuleius, who attended a gathering of the cult of Isis in the second century AD, observed that a "multiform crown, consisting of various flowers, bound the sublime summit of her head. And in the middle of the crown there was a smooth orb resembling a mirror, or rather a white refulgent light which indicated that she was the moon."

The story of Isis, as recounted by the Greek historian Plutarch, centers on the loss of her husband-brother Osiris, who is slain by his sibling Set. Isis wanders in search of Osiris's body and eventually brings about his rebirth through magical incantations. The annual flooding of the Nile and the subsequent "rebirth" of inundated farmlands came to be associated with the death and resurrection of Osiris. The cult of Isis spread among the Greeks and the Romans, who referred to her as Hecate and Ceres.

A typical incantation to Isis was found in a papyrus from the first century AD that had been recorded by a magician identified only as N. N., who noted he had invoked the goddess for an evil purpose. Though tediously extensive, the recitation captures the intensity of Egyptian magical ceremonies: "I invoke you, ye holy ones, mighty, majestic, glorious Splendours, holy and earth-born, mighty archdaimons; compeers of the great god, denizens of Chaos, of Erebus and of the unfathomable abyss; earth-dwellers, haunter of sky-depths, nook-infesting, murk-enwrapped; scanning the mysteries, guardians of secrets, captains of the hosts of hell; kings of infinite space, terrestrial overlords, globe-shaking, firm-founding, ministering to earthquakes; terror-strangling, panic-striking, spindle turning; snow-scattering, rain-wafters, spirits of air; fire-tongues of summer-sun, tempest-tossing lords of fate; dark shapes of Erebus, senders of necessity; flame-fanning fire darters; snow compelling, dew-compelling; gale-raising abyss-plumbing, calm-bestriding air-spirits; dauntless in courage, heart-crushing despots; chasm-leaping, overburdening, iron-nerved daimons; wild ranging, unenslaved; watchers of Tartaros; delusive fate-phantoms; all-seeing, all-hearing, all-conquering, sky-wandering vagrants; life-inspiring, life destroying, primeval pole-movers; heart-jocund death-dealers; revealers of angels, justicers of mortals, sunless revealers, masters of daimons, air-roving, omnipotent, holy, invincible . . ."—here, several secret magic words were left to the magus to discover—"perform my behest."

N. N. admonished that the incantation could be spoken only after a period of ritual preparation, during which the magician pledged himself to purity, sobriety, and chastity. For some reason, the magus was also required to refrain from bathing during the preparations. The papyrus specifies that robes of clean linen be worn for the ceremony and prescribes recipes for incense along with various magic symbols. The latter might include such items as "a hair of a virgin ox, blue shimmering female corpse with legs apart, and the transfixed privy parts of a female monkey."

In every case, the instructions were precise. No less so were the magician's directions for consecrating himself before the invocation of the goddess: "Keep yourself pure for seven days, and then go on the third day of the moon to a place which the receding Nile has just laid bare. Make a fire on two upright bricks with olive-wood when the sun is half-risen, after having before sunrise circumambulated the altar. But when the sun's disc is clear above the horizon, decapitate an immaculate, pure white cock, holding it in the crook of your left elbow; circumambulate the altar before sunrise. Hold the cock fast by your knees and decapitate it with no one else holding it. Throw the head into the river, catch the blood in your right hand and drink it up. Put the rest of the body on the burning altar and jump into the river. Dive under in

the clothes you are wearing, then stepping backwards climb on to the bank. Put on new clothes and go away without turning around. After that take the gall of a raven and rub some of it with the wing of an ibis on your eyes and you will be consecrated."

As a final touch, the magician was instructed

to draw a feather, the sign of truth, upon his tongue in green ink. Then, in a color chosen to please the deity of the hour, he would trace a circle on the earth. And within the circle the invocation could at last be performed. The incongruity of magicians preparing themselves through purity and abstinence to claim the magic powers to kill, torture, or satiate their lusts may or may not have been lost on the author of the papyrus. But it was perfectly in keeping with the traditions of ritual magic that derived from the Egyptian customs. The point—at least in the eyes of the magus—was that he would be calling on a god or goddess to help him achieve his ends.

Following the Egyptian model, magicians throughout history have performed their rites within the bounds of a circle. The shape is used, among other things, to symbolize the universe and the procreative process of life and regeneration. Its use in ritual can be understood in terms of imitative magic: The circle becomes a sort of stage that is the model of the universe. What transpires within the circle will take effect in the greater universe, as long as the magician hews to tradition and speaks all the words correctly. Egyptian tradition also originated the practice of including other geometric shapes within the boundaries of a magic circle to protect the activities of the magician and the safety of other participants. The pentagram, or five-pointed star, for example, was believed to be potent in thwarting hostile spirits who might take it upon themselves to overturn a ceremony.

From the Egyptians, ceremonial magic seems to have spread to Europe through disparate channels. The three primary conduits were Greek Pythagoreanism, a cultic movement called Gnosticism, and the Jewish cabalistic tradition. Pythagoreanism revolved around the ideas that everything recurs eternally and that numbers carry a mystical significance. The Gnostics were members of a variety of cults that blossomed in centuries just before and after the time of Christ. They believed that all earthly matter was evil and that salvation could be attained only through the pursuit of certain esoteric spiritual truths. Cabalism was marked by the belief that everything in the world came about through a gradual process of emanation from the Godhead. Adherents studied several highly complicated systems for interpreting scripture by means of ciphers, or codes. These traditions shared certain common elements, and at various times, each attracted devoted followings. Of the three, the Jewish magical Cabala was probably the most influential.

The term *Cabala* derives from the Hebrew word for tradition. Like most of the occult systems within the European tradition of high magic, the Cabala included spells designed to induce an unseen population of spirits to carry out the magician's wishes. The interpretations of the Old Testament upon which the spells were based purportedly had their start in the verbal instructions of the patriarch Abraham to a select group of followers. The folklore of the Cabala holds that the rituals and secrets were passed along orally from one generation to the next until they were written down by King Solomon. The monarch is said to have employed the secret powers in building the first great temple of Jerusalem. To create that fabled structure, he allegedly conjured up an army of spirits and set them to work cutting and placing marble blocks.

Historians tend to place the beginnings of the Cabala in a considerably later framework. The earliest date that most scholars accept is the third century AD, when the oldest known text was produced. This work, called the *Sefer Yezira,* combined elements of Gnostic spirit worship with the central interpretive apparatus of the Cabala, which springs from the notion that secret messages are hidden in every letter, number, and accent mark of the Pentateuch, the first five books of the Old Testament. A later text, the *Clavicula Salomonis,* or *Key of Solomon,* was passed off by its authors as King Solomon's contribution, reflecting the magical secrets that he shared with his own chosen few. Scholars suspect, however, that the text was actually written sometime in the fifteenth century.

Practitioners used a variety of different methods for tweaking out the hidden contents of the Old Testament. The

simplest, called *gematria,* was based on a system in which each of the twenty-two letters in the Hebrew alphabet was assigned a numerical value. Thus, any word could be substituted for any other as long as they both had the same total numerical value. A phrase from Genesis such as "And behold three men" could also be construed to mean "These are Michael, Gabriel, and Raphael." The second method, *notarikon,* took a two-directional approach. The interpreter either used each letter from a single word as the initial letters in a group of words that formed a sentence, or reversed the stratagem, using a number of initial letters to compose a key word. Following the latter course, "Ate Gibor Leilam Adonai" (Thou art mighty forever, O Lord) yields the mystical word *AGLA,* believed to be a name for God. *Temura,* a more complex, third method of interpretation, employed a host of permutations and letter combinations to root out the ciphers left by God in the passages of the Old Testament.

A constant subject of speculation for early Cabala devo-

tees was the true pronunciation of the Tetragrammaton, commonly referred to as "the word of four letters." This was the unutterable name of Jehovah, which purportedly carried great power and danger. Presented in the scriptures by the Hebrew letters *Yod He Vau He,* or *YHVH,* the word was believed to have been in general circulation during Old Testament times, but knowledge of its exact pronunciation had been lost in the decades following the collapse of the Jewish kingdom. With no vowels in the Hebrew alphabet to guide the uninformed speaker, the magicians were at a loss to put to use this most powerful of words. At one point in the third century AD, Cabalists claimed to

Catherine de Médicis, queen consort of Henry II of France in the sixteenth century, avidly believed in the powers of magic despite her Catholic upbringing. She made no decisions— public or private—without first consulting a bevy of astrologers and magicians.

Devices to Tap the Unseen Power

Although their aim was to transcend the physical realm, some ritual magicians had an eye for the sublime when it came to their worldly trappings. Surely, it must have seemed, if a scrap of mirror or a small sphere of glass could reveal the future to Gypsy diviners, then a beautifully contoured looking glass or a fine crystal orb would do the job all the better. Many conjurers therefore set themselves apart with elaborate costumes, talismans, and wands. Some magicians, no doubt, also found it reassuring that they could dazzle at least their mortal observers if the spirits proved slow to respond to their calls or ignored their entreaties altogether.

Pictured here is a sampling of treasured accouterments left behind by magicians of various eras.

This French crystal ball, about four inches in diameter, guided eighteenth-century magicians in their forecasts. The diviners attempted to draw into the ball informative images or visitors from the spirit world.

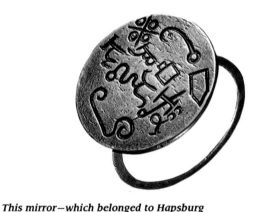

A seventeenth-century magus wore this lunar amulet ring to garner good health and respect. Cast in silver, the metal traditionally associated with the moon, the ring is engraved with astrological symbols.

This mirror—which belonged to Hapsburg archduke Ferdinand of Tyrol, a collector of alleged magical objects—reflects a slightly different distorted image from each convex glass. Magicians have long used mirrors to probe reality's secrets.

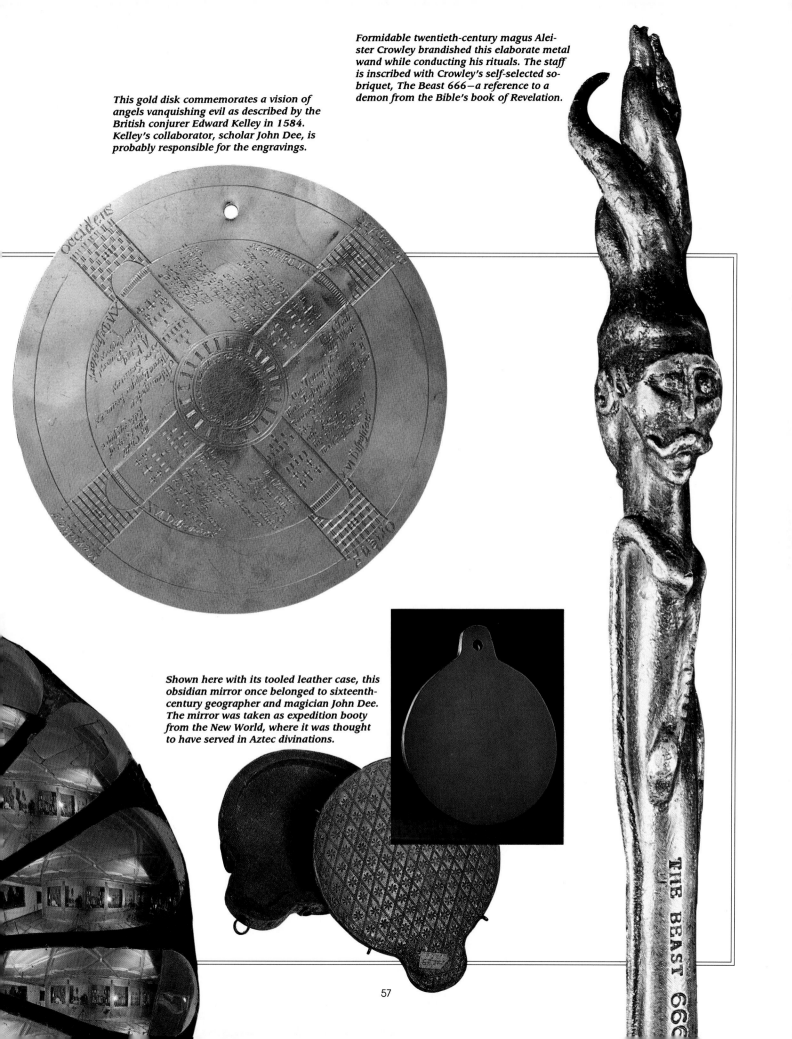

This gold disk commemorates a vision of angels vanquishing evil as described by the British conjurer Edward Kelley in 1584. Kelley's collaborator, scholar John Dee, is probably responsible for the engravings.

Formidable twentieth-century magus Aleister Crowley brandished this elaborate metal wand while conducting his rituals. The staff is inscribed with Crowley's self-selected sobriquet, The Beast 666—a reference to a demon from the Bible's book of Revelation.

Shown here with its tooled leather case, this obsidian mirror once belonged to sixteenth-century geographer and magician John Dee. The mirror was taken as expedition booty from the New World, where it was thought to have served in Aztec divinations.

57

have rediscovered the pronunciation. They jealously guarded that knowledge, however, and the debate continued.

Key of Solomon became the most popular guide to cabalistic wisdom for magicians of the Middle Ages. It continued to be greatly prized centuries later because it explicitly detailed all manner of ritual practices. Here again, as in Egyptian tradition, the magus was required to maintain chastity and abstinence before enacting rituals. He might also feel obliged to pray, meditate, or carry out elaborate ablutions before undertaking a ceremony. *Key* stipulated that the starting times for ceremonies be set by careful observation of astrological tables. As for locations, the book advised magicians to seek out places that were "concealed, removed and separated from the habitations of men, such as the borders of lakes, forests, dark and obscure places, old and deserted houses, whither rarely and scarce ever men do come; mountains, caves, caverns, grottoes, gardens, orchards; but best of all are cross-roads, and where four roads meet, during the depth and silence of the night."

The costume of the magus was also spelled out explicitly in the pages of *Key of Solomon*. He was to wear white linen, every thread of which had been spun by a virgin. Certain symbols were to be embroidered upon the robes, and the magus was to provide himself with a metal pentagram, which would strike terror in the spirits and reduce them to obedience. Pentagrams were to be inscribed with symbolic designs and worn by the magicians "before their breasts, consecrated, and covered with a silken veil and perfumed with the proper fumigation."

The magus also had to forge his own sword, knife, poniard, lancet, and needle. This smithing was to take place under prescribed astrological conditions and be carried out, in some cases, with special ingredients. For example, tools were to be tempered with the blood of a magpie, a gosling, or a mole, depending on the nature of the instrument. Knife handles, on the other hand, were to be made from boxwood cut with a single stroke of a newly made sword.

With such arcana, the would-be magician's labors were only beginning. There were blood sacrifices to be made of lambs and goats, inks and incenses to be prepared, and endless purification procedures, all leading to the final moment of conjuration when a spirit could be ushered, defanged and acquiescent, across the boundary separating the living and the dead. Once delivered, the powers of the spirit would be deemed to be at the disposal of the magus.

As in Egyptian ritual, the magician was required to draw a magic circle with his consecrated sword. Devotees of cabalism made the creation of circles into a minor art form, and *Key of Solomon* dutifully presented elaborate instructions on useful inscriptions and adornments to be included. The one element certain to appear, however, was the Hebrew calligraphy representing the unpronounceable name of God. With the site of the ceremony thus fully prepared, the magician could at last begin to recite his spells within the circumscribed space.

A passage from *Key* describes a typical ritual: "After having said all these words devoutly, let the Master arise, and place his hand upon the Pentagrams, and let one of the Companions hold the Book open before the Master, who, raising his eyes to heaven, and turning unto the Four Quarters of the Universe, shall say: 'O Lord, be Thou unto me a Tower of Strength against the appearance and assault of Evil Spirits.' After this, turning towards the Four Quarters of the Universe, he shall say the following words: 'These be the Symbols and the Names of the Creator, which can bring Terror and Fear unto you. Obey me then, by the power of these Holy Names and by these Mysterious Symbols of the Secret of Secrets.' The which being said and done, thou shalt see them draw near and approach from all parts."

With that, the magus could expect the appearance of spirits. He was instructed in *Key of Solomon* to uncover the pentagram hidden at his breast and command the spirits "with an assured air and a grave and imperious voice" to be tranquil. To back up the request, he might renew his fumigations by tossing a quantity of incense on the fire. Once he had put away the pentagram, he could expect to witness wonderful things of a kind impossible to relate. Then the king of the spirits would grant whatever wishes the magician chose to relate.

During the turbulent centuries from the end of the Roman Empire to the Renaissance, the rituals of the Cabala became ever more intertwined with other magical systems that managed to survive as Christianity spread across Europe. The most influential of these traditions were Pythagorean numerology, alchemical sorcery, and the herbalistic magic developed by the wandering scholar Paracelsus. The talismanic magic of the Gypsies also came to be practiced side by side with the rituals of the Cabala. In fact, all of these forms of magic seemed to take a free hand in adopting the lore and customs of the others.

Pythagoras, who was born in Greece around 580 BC, provided the basis for many of the numerological beliefs used by high magicians. His followers, who called themselves a brotherhood, developed rites of initiation and observed rigid behavioral constraints. Their secrets were built up around a group of mathematical formulations first framed by Pythagoras but later expanded to embrace—at least in theory—all aspects of human existence. A great deal of ingenuity and mathematical insight went into Pythagoras's theorems, so they had a wide appeal for magicians working in other traditions. Most popular was a process for obtaining the mathematical equivalents of words according to a scale in which each letter of the Greek and Hebrew alphabets was assigned a numerical value.

The Gnostics believed, among other things, that the world was controlled by an evil archon, who was none other than the God of the Old Testament. They pursued salvation along two opposite paths: Some embraced extreme asceticism and others flagrant licentiousness. Eventually, they came to weave a mystical terminology for their beliefs from a web of Pythagorean numerology. For example, they believed the word *abraxas* had magical powers that could be detected numerologically by summing up the numerical

The Ambivalent Magus

A leader of the occult revival in the mid-to-late 1800s, Éliphas Lévi has been called the last of the magi. Oddly enough, he was never an active practitioner of magic, preferring the role of theoretician or teacher. He believed magicians could harness the strength of the human will but shunned doing so himself because he considered magic morally and physically dangerous.

Christened Alphonse Louis Constant in Paris in 1810, he would eventually adopt the Hebrew equivalent of his given names. He was the son of a poor shoemaker and was educated free of charge by his local Catholic parish. Thus embraced by the Church, he decided to become a priest. His training ended, however, when he was expelled for too freely speaking his mind.

Young Constant threw himself into radical politics and was jailed several times for his activities. He was married for seven years, but the relationship deteriorated and he turned heart and soul to a study of the occult. Refusing to acknowledge his split with Catholicism, he became absorbed in the teachings of Swedish philosopher Emanuel Swedenborg. He studied the Cabala and the Tarot and was the first to propose a link between the two. He took to wearing clerical garb and called himself the Abbé Constant, while earning a living as a teacher of magic.

In the mid-1850s, he began writing under the name Magus Éliphas Lévi. His works have proved surprisingly durable; they still exert their influence more than a century after Lévi's death in 1875.

values of the Greek letters from which it was composed: Letting alpha equal 1, beta equal 2, rho equal 100, alpha equal 1, xi equal 60, alpha equal 1, and sigma equal 200, the sum came to 365—the number of days in a year. The Gnostics believed that there was a spirit for each of those days.

Other important numbers were 360, which described the full circle of the year, and 5, which corresponded to the five classes of creatures that Gnostics believed inhabited the earth. The numerologists observed that 360 is divisible by 5, exactly 72 times. And 72 is one of the most sacred of all numbers; it is a part of cabalistic numerology and is referred to in the Old Testament. These and other more sophisticated mathematical formulations became an integral part of magical ceremonies throughout Europe.

Another strain of magic that became part of the heritage of men like Cagliostro and John Dee was the ancient practice of alchemy. In its most familiar form, alchemy involved the effort to create gold from baser metals. In contrast to most other forms of high magic, it was largely a private pursuit, carried out in laboratories by the precursors of modern chemists. The quest for man-made gold actually led to the discovery of a few important chemical compounds, such as Glauber's salt, which is used in dyeing processes. But alchemists pursued a variety of other objectives as well, including eternal life and spiritual perfection.

The earliest roots of alchemy are not fully known. It seems to have sprung up in roughly similar forms in the Orient and the Middle East. Whether the two beginnings were related has been a subject for debate among historians. But for Western alchemists, the craft had its start in the writings of the legendary figure Hermes Trismegistus.

ermes is referred to in some alchemical texts as a deity who took human form and reigned as king of Egypt in the third millennium BC. He was associated with Thoth, the Egyptian god of learning, language, and writing. The Greeks equated Thoth with their own deity Hermes, and they considered Hermes to be the author of many important books on magic. The few remaining texts purported to be his are heavily allegorical. One tract, the Emerald Table, was allegedly discovered in an ancient Egyptian tomb. In some accounts, the finder was Alexander the Great.

The Emerald Table is a marvel of indirection that lends itself to nearly endless interpretation. "Tis true, without falsehood, and most real," the work begins, "that which is above is like that which is below. And as all things have been derived from one, by the thought of one, so all things are born from this thing by adoption." It goes on to instruct the would-be alchemist to separate earth from fire and the subtle from the gross.

Scholars do not know the true origins of the Emerald Table. The earliest printed version appeared in 1541, but it claimed to be based on writings more than 300 years older. For centuries, alchemists followed the precepts contained in the Emerald Table, performing countless sulfurous reductions in smoky laboratories hung with pentagrams. As time passed, interest in alchemy rose and fell, and the interests of its practitioners swung repeatedly from gold to elixirs of life to spiritual growth and back to gold. Its arts were studied by swindlers and holy men alike, but whatever the intentions of the magicians, the laboratory processes and rituals passed down as tradition continued to be observed.

While occult systems such as alchemy and the Cabala had long and convoluted histories, the wandering scholars who studied them had no monopoly on the practice of magic. A multitude of simpler, more mechanical methods of hexing, healing, divining, and bewitching sprang up in every corner of society. Talismans, potions, and all manner of incense were used by common folk in hopes of attracting or controlling spirits. A typical concoction to repel hostile spirits might include sulfur, myrrh, red sandalwood, rotten apples, vinegar, wine galls, and arsenic. To some extent, this magic rooted in folklore was adopted by the professional magicians and became a part of their rituals. The opposite also held true, as the customs of low magic were shaped by the bits and pieces of occult knowledge that sifted down to the general population. Nevertheless, stories abound of folk magicians who attempted to steal the thunder of the high priests and got in over their heads.

One such episode came to light on Christmas day in 1715 on the outskirts of the quiet German town of Jena, when the bodies of two dead men and the nearly lifeless body of a third were discovered in a small hut adjacent to a vineyard. The victims, covered with welts and bruises, were surrounded by bizarre paraphernalia that clearly had been part of some sort of occult ceremony. The survivor—a student named Weber—was later taken to court to provide an account of the tragedy.

According to his story, one of the dead men, a peasant named Gessner, had suspected that there was treasure buried in the vineyard and had enlisted the aid of the other two in conjuring a spirit to locate the trove. Weber was not trained in magic, but he had been recruited because he possessed several books on the subject, including *Key of Solomon* and *Harrowing of Hell*. The latter was a tract written—so it claimed—by the legendary wizard Johann Faust. The third man, Zenner, had a mandrake root that he had hoped to put to some magical purpose. The three men perused Weber's books for some time and concluded that a sun spirit called Nathael was guarding the treasure.

After darkness fell on Christmas Eve, they equipped themselves with pentagrams and lanterns and headed out to the vineyard. There, dispensing with the usual time-consuming steps of

ritual purification, they commenced to perform an invocation as described in one of Weber's texts. They wrote the Tetragrammaton on the door of the hut, enkindled a small charcoal fire in a pot, and traced a magic circle on the ceiling. At about ten o'clock, Gessner began the conjuring in earnest, reciting three times an incantation he deemed suitable. Weber followed with passages from *Harrowing of Hell*, which included references to Adonai, *AGLA*, Jehovah, and other divine names. He then made an

Seeker of the Inner Light

British occultist and novelist Mary Violet Firth was better known as Dion Fortune, a play on one of her mottoes, "Deo non fortuna," or "By God, not luck."

Born in 1891, Firth was brought up a Christian Scientist and attributed her early interest in the supernatural to church founder Mary Baker Eddy. But she also recounted a brush with disaster at the age of nineteen that led her to turn to the occult. In 1910, Firth claimed, she was the victim of a "psychic attack." It seems that her boss put her under such severe stress that she suffered a nervous breakdown. But Firth was convinced the damage went much deeper: She claimed her boss had attacked her on the astral plane and drained Firth's astral body of its vital energy. In restoring herself to health, Firth studied the psychoanalytic theories of Freud and Jung. In 1919, she joined the Alpha and Omega Lodge of the Stella Matutina, an offshoot of a group of occultists called the Hermetic Order of the Golden Dawn. Under the guidance of leader J. W. Brodie-Innes, Firth cultivated magical powers of her own. By 1924, she had established a secret order, the Fraternity of the Inner Light, which she directed until her death in 1946. Firth promulgated an esoteric approach to the practice of magic that she described as a "revival of the ancient Temple Mysteries." She published numerous books, including *Psychic Self-Defense.*

invocation to Och, the Prince of the Kingdom of the Sun. Och was invited to send his servant Nathael to help the men find the treasure. It was then, Weber claimed, that darkness rose before him and he collapsed in a stupor.

When Weber was discovered, he was still unconscious on the floor, flanked by the bodies of his companions. Asphyxiation was immediately suspected, but there was nothing obvious to explain the violent deaths of Zenner and Gessner. The welts and scratch marks on their bodies could hardly have been the result of noxious fumes. Officials in Jena undertook what they considered a sober-minded examination of the evidence. They were unable, however, to discern any rational explanation and arrived at the disquieting conclusion that the tragedy had come about because of the slipshod manner in which the victims had conducted their ritual. It was conjectured that the unskilled magicians had unleashed forces beyond their power to control.

Whether or not the townsfolk of Jena fell prey to mass hysteria is now impossible to know, but the tragedy continued to unfold. Three watchmen were stationed at the vineyard to investigate the incident. A day later, they were found in the same condition as the three would-be magicians; one was dead and the other two were clinging to life. In the hut, *Harrowing of Hell* still lay open on the table. The survivors testified that their only recollections were of the spirit of a small boy who had scratched at the door and then glided into the hut.

Many episodes live on in the lore of magic that are comparable to the occurrences at Jena. For centuries, mysterious deaths were routinely blamed on forces of the occult, usually for lack of any better explanation. There were also many clear-cut cases in which magicians were killed in accidents involving the misuse of dangerous fumigations and potions—though far fewer such deaths than were caused by the medical procedures of the times. Paracelsus, the sixteenth-century alchemist and physician, eschewed most of the medical practices of his day in favor of herbal magic and treatments of his own devising. "Doctors of medicine," he wrote, "should consider better what they plainly see, that for instance an unlettered peasant heals more than all of them with all their books and red gowns."

Although Paracelsus sometimes made his remedies a part of arcane magical ceremonies, he explored some important scientific ideas. More than a century before William Harvey was credited with discovering the workings of the circulatory system, Paracelsus was describing "the sap of life." He also discovered the painkilling attributes of the opium derivatives called laudanum, which eventually came into widespread use. And he was one of the first to experiment with mercury in treating venereal disease.

But the time in which scholarly mavericks like Paracelsus could devote the bulk of their energies to occult pursuits and still hold their own in the legitimate sciences would eventually come to an end. During the eighteenth and nineteenth centuries, advances in medicine and other branches of science began to strip away the mystique that had always surrounded high magic. As more and more aspects of human existence became approachable in purely scientific terms, the high priests of magic were slowly but surely relieved of their aura of power. During this era of gradual decline, an old and particularly perverse element of high magic took on renewed importance.

The history of magic has always been rife with tales of sexual exploitation. As recounted in the literature of the occult, women were occasionally stripped, raped, beaten, and even skinned and sacrificed in the fulfillment of magicians' perverse appetites. The old magical texts contain spells designed to obtain the sexual acquiescence of women; some also describe rituals in which women play a role, usually in some erotic function. But as the sorcerers lost their authority over astronomy, chemistry, and medicine, they must have realized that sexuality was one of the few remaining areas in which they could justly claim to know as much as anyone else. They made sex a more central feature of ceremonial magic. In the thrall of sexual excitement, the magicians claimed, transcendent powers were concentrated in the magus. Thus charged, he could better administer a rite.

For theory to justify this use of sex, occultists turned to the East and the Tantric practices of Hinduism and Buddhism. There they found a ready-made tradition of sexual magic and copious instructions for its implementation.

In contrast to the relative asceticism of orthodox Hindu and Buddhist belief, Tantric spiritualism holds that through the use of pleasure—specifically erotic pleasure—humans make contact with the divine. The essential idea of Tantrism is that all human experience is the result of the interplay between a female creative principle, embodied in a goddess of many forms known as Shakti, and a male principle, identified with the god Shiva. The interplay of these principles is inherently sexual, and by approximating it in intercourse, Tantrists, or believers, can transform themselves into the two coupling divinities. In doing so, adherents believe, they achieve a higher state of consciousness and come to personify the workings of the universe at large.

Tantrists pursued this transformation through sex, meditation, drugs, and magic. They thought of the human body as comprising various sections, called *chakras,* each possessing distinctive properties and being cared for in special ways. By assuming various yogic postures and having sex in different coital positions, Tantrists attempted to release the energy contained in every part of their bodies. In this fashion, they hoped to elevate themselves to an enlightened state. In the version of Tantrism most widely adopted by Western ceremonial magicians, the sex act was prolonged as long as possible in hopes of creating a buildup of sexual energy that would lift the participants to altered states of consciousness. One ancient Chinese text described this as the path to immortality. According to the theory, the male participant would attempt to bring his partner to orgasm without ejaculating himself, so as to assimilate the woman's life force without relinquishing his own. If he was able to accomplish this act with ten different women a night for enough nights, he could expect eventually to obtain eternal life.

At least in its Western manifestations, ritual sex has been notable chiefly as a measure of the cynicism of the magicians advocating its use. But then, cynicism, exploitation, and outright fraud seem never to have been in short supply throughout the history of ceremonial magic—and certainly not in the last hundred years.

Interest in the occult actually underwent a significant revival in the final decades of the nineteenth century. Secret magical societies such as the Order of the Temple of the Orient and the Rosicrucians came into their own and attracted widespread attention. In France, men like writer Éliphas Lévi and the Abbé Boullan, who founded an occult group called the Church of Carmel, also stirred new interest in magic. The Hermetic Order of the Golden Dawn was just one of many occult groups that sprang up in England during those years. It brought together ardent students of the arcane arts, such as Aleister Crowley and Samuel Liddell MacGregor Mathers, with well-known writers such as Bram Stoker, Algernon Blackwood, and William Butler Yeats. Members translated the old grimoires, delved into theories of numerology, and developed original rituals and spells.

As ceremonial magic entered the twentieth century, it found a public still hungry for spiritualism. The continued attraction of the occult arts is not easily explained away. Some observers believe that ritual magic simply fills a void for some people who may have abandoned their orthodox religious beliefs in the face of expanded scientific understanding of human existence. The author G. K. Chesterton subscribed to this view. Writing at the turn of the century, he noted that for many people who lose their faith in Christianity, the alternative to believing in nothing is to believe in anything at all. So perhaps even if the convoluted rigors of formal ceremonial magic are too arcane or off-putting for most people, they may always find some disciples.

The current followers tend to be a highly fragmented group. Working alone or in small bands, occultists devote themselves to a variety of magical specialties, including Egyptian, Celtic, and Nordic customs and a version of the Cabala interwoven with Christian ideas. By far the liveliest area of occult interest during the 1980s and early 1990s has been an updated form of witchcraft called Wicca, after the Old English word for *sorcerer*. This movement, which claims to be a revival of a pre-Christian nature religion that venerated a supreme goddess, involves its adherents in a year-round cycle of rituals marking everything from marriages and births to the passing of the seasons and Halloween. Wiccans are loosely confederated and notably freewheeling in their revisions of the standard rituals. Like other occult movements, however, they take a surprisingly ambivalent attitude toward magic.

For many of the latter-day witches, magic is secondary to other aspects of their adopted religion. Far more significant, for some, is the act of turning away from the male gods of conventional religions in favor of a transcendent female deity. For others, the primary attraction is Wicca's pantheistic worship of the spirits in nature—a stance they find environmentally sound. For some Wiccans, therefore, the practice of magic and questions regarding its efficacy are all but irrelevant. The same can be said for many students of other occult systems: They are druids or shamans or Cabalists first, and magicians only incidentally.

But if the heyday of the magi is past, many of the ancillary aspects of high magic appear to be going strong. Collectively known as low magic, these include popular astrology, talisman worship, palm reading, voodoo, and a wide variety of magical healing techniques. This lore attracts millions of followers and probably constitutes the most widespread strain of magic in evidence today.

"World's Wickedest Man"

Edward Alexander (Aleister) Crowley dedicated his life to the reintroduction of "magick." He used the old spelling to set his craft apart from newer forms of conjuring, which he believed were debased. Crowley claimed to be the prophet of a new eon—one revealed to him by his guardian angel. Following the great ages of paganism and Christianity, it would be ruled by the power of the human will, or Thelema, rather than by external gods. A single dictum would prevail: "Do what thou wilt shall be the whole of the Law."

Whatever his pretentions, Crowley's life amounted to a long struggle to tear away the strictures of conventional morality. He chafed at his strict upbringing and did his utmost to distance himself from his fundamentalist-Christian roots. In his twenties, he joined the Hermetic Order of the Golden Dawn. He discovered tantric yoga and cultivated theories on the potential benefits of sex and drugs. To pursue such ideas, he founded the Order of the Silver Star and, in 1920, established an abbey in Sicily. There, he and his companions dedicated themselves to the practice of sexual magic.

Within three years, however, Crowley was expelled from Italy. When he returned to England, he had become a scandalous figure and was a favored target for the London tabloids. Headlines denounced him as "the wickedest man in the world." In the 1930s, he was financially ruined, but he continued to write and publish until his death in 1947. His ashes were shipped to disciples in the United States.

Practitioners of an Ancient Craft

When I was a young man, I went up on Heart Butte and fasted and prayed for seven days. I was dressed in very old clothes and continually called upon the sun to have pity on me. At last, the sun appeared before me as a very old man, gave me a drum and one song." Thus did a Blackfoot shaman recount his initiation, a solitary ordeal resulting in a vision that brought him spiritual power. In such a vision, warned an Australian shaman, "You may see dead persons walking towards you, and you will hear their bones rattle. If you hear and see these things without fear, you will never be frightened of anything. You are now powerful because you have seen these dead people."

Medicine men and women all over the world practice shamanism, earth's earliest religion, and in doing so employ ritual magic as a tool. In the shamanic world-view, spirits inhabit and rule all things, visible and invisible, and it is vital to be on good terms with them. Terrifying initiation visions qualify the shaman as a tribe's spiritual leader, soothsayer, doctor, judge, artist, and master of ceremonies. Many aspiring shamans court such visions through days of fasting and sleeplessness, self-flagellation, and hallucinogenic herbs. "You see, these tests are to teach my people how to live," said a medicine woman from California's Pomo tribe. "On the way," she added, "you're going to suffer."

The photographs that appear on the following pages, all taken around the turn of the century, record the shaman's role in traditional Native American cultures.

Tek-'ic, a shaman of the Alaskan Tlingit tribe, sits for his portrait with his long hair reaching the step on which his feet rest. Many shamans let their hair grow uncut for decades, believing it to be a source of their magical power. Tek-'ic's wood-and-feather headdress was exclusive to his mystical station.

Guides in the Quest for Nature's Favor

Much of the shaman's magic was aimed at securing the tribe's survival. Every aspect of weather—drenching spring thunderstorms, crop-withering droughts, and the nurturing warmth of the sun—was seen as a manifestation of spirit powers. Tribal peoples felt duty-bound to keep these powers in balance through right living.

As the repository of tribal lore, the shaman offered guidance in correct spiritual conduct. Although the methods varied according to the situation, tribe, and deity, the shaman chose and prescribed or conducted rituals for every eventuality. Many were simple, personal rites, such as the Comanche custom of offering a morsel of food heavenward during a formal meal, then burying it. At the other extreme was the occasional Pawnee sacrifice of a human being, a young woman captive from another tribe. The maiden, who was ritually killed with an arrow through her heart, represented the deity Evening Star; her heavenly reunion with her husband, Morning Star, so the members of the tribe believed, magically renewed the fertility of the whole earth.

Among the Pueblo—Southwestern growers of corn, beans, and squash—shamans presided over a sixteen-day winter-solstice ceremony that culminated in the blessing of the seed corn. The Hopi, another Southwestern planter tribe, entrusted spring rainmaking to their shamanic Snake Society. These men danced with rattlesnakes in their mouths and then freed them in the hope that they would ask the gods to send rain.

High on a bluff near the Rio Grande, a lone Pueblo Indian presents a daybreak offering of cornmeal to the spirits of the clouds and sun. Several tribes of the Southwest made such offerings in petitioning for warm winds and plentiful rain.

Knowledgeable Wielders of Sacred Tools

Generally, tribes followed a shaman's every instruction regarding ceremonies, in deference to his superior knowledge. Shamans of many tribes could forecast the winter and summer solstices and timed planting or hunting festivals to coincide with them. Although predicting solar or lunar eclipses was beyond the means of Native American astronomy, shamans knew about these celestial events and responded with rituals, such as the dance at right, to forestall their ill effects.

Shamans derived authority not only from their knowledge but from their impressive appearance. They wore ornate headdresses and robes decorated with hoofs, tails, toes, and skins of animals seen in visions, magical helpers whose cries the shaman might mimic when invoking their powers in spells, chants, and dances.

Shamans also relied on certain knives, rattles, and natural objects that symbolized their power. These ritual tools were handled with utmost ceremony and kept in a "medicine bundle." The bundles and the objects of power within them were thought too potent for the uninitiated even to touch. After one Papago shaman died suddenly, leaving his medicine bundle in a woodshed, his widow asked another medicine man to come and remove it, so that she could feel safe fetching firewood from the shed. In the meantime, she let a researcher examine the bundle's contents, which were found to be two deer tails, four quartz crystals, some eagle down, and an eagle claw. The widow hid her family in the house during this unveiling and afterward never spoke to the researcher again.

Following a shaman's commands, Kwakiutl tribesmen of northwestern Canada dance around a fire in this 1910 ceremony to save the eclipsed moon from being devoured by the Mouth of Heaven. Their shaman explained that the foul-smelling smoke from their fire, fueled with hair and old clothing, made the sky creature sneeze and disgorge its prize.

Dispensers of Strong Medicine

Like all else in the Native Americans' world, sickness had its spiritual or magical causes. It might be brought on by a witch's spell or a broken taboo. Since an illness or wound meant that the sacred balance between humans and the spirits had been upset, the shaman was often called in to restore the spirits' goodwill and heal the patient.

Healing rituals took different forms according to the specific ailment and the particular tribe. In the simplest treatments, the shaman might massage the patient and then blow or suck on the afflicted part of the body as other clan members looked on. Many shamans would eventually show the patient some natural object—a twig or a crystal—explaining that it had come out of the patient's body and was the cause of the complaint. At least one shaman acknowledged that sleight of hand was involved. "We could heal without it," he said, "but the people need something to see."

More complex healing ceremonies required chants and fetishes, and even sacred artistry. Navajo shamans made holy sand drawings on the ground and laid their patients atop them to effect the cure. In serious witchcraft cases, in which the shaman diagnosed the theft of a patient's soul, a team of shamans might be called in to find the soul and rescue it. Shamans of the Pacific Northwest performed this service in pantomime, paddling an imaginary canoe to a remote hiding place where spirits held the lost soul captive. Once they had retrieved the soul, the shamans mimed its return to the patient, to the noise of rattles and chants.

Five Pueblo shamans try to exorcise a boy's disease, shaking rattles and calling to the spirits that they believe have entered the child (foreground) and made him ill. On the ground in front of the shamans are the fetishes, in this case medicine bundles, that are thought to hold their magical powers.

Guarantors of a Successful Hunt

A shaman's good standing in a community of hunters often depended on his skill at providing game, especially among tribes for whom hunger and pestilence were frequent visitors. The Tlingit of Alaska assumed it was the shaman who magically brought forth bounties of fish. In parts of the American West, shamans envisioned approaching game herds in trances and dreams. Tribal hunts for antelope or other big-game animals rarely proceeded without the inspiration of such visions.

But contact with the supernatural was not the province of the shaman alone. Even the humblest tribal member could address the spirit forces. Among the Mandan along the upper Missouri River, anyone could fast or make offerings to bring buffalo, the tribe's principal source of food. Following the shaman's spiritual instructions, a leader of a Mandan hunting party performed simple rites before the hunt, praying to the buffalo spirit and tying an offering of sage and eagle feathers to the horns of any nearby buffalo skull.

Many hunters relied on animal spirit helpers to point the way to the game. The Comanche believed the horned toad would run off in the direction of the buffalo. The Cheyenne were convinced a cricket placed in the palm of a hunter's hand would point its antennae toward the herd. When a hunt was successful, there were magical precautions to ensure that nature's sustenance would continue. Shamans taught Apache hunters to turn the head of a freshly killed and skinned animal toward the east, the sacred direction from which the sun came to replenish life.

On the plains of North Dakota, a Mandan offers a bleached buffalo skull to the animal's spirit in the hope of securing a successful hunt. Such a skull was considered a powerful part of a Mandan medicine bundle.

CHAPTER 3

Low Road to Personal Gain

The Algonquin chieftain had been in the agonies of love from the moment he laid eyes on the beautiful young Frenchwoman in the frontier village of Kaskaskia, Illinois. All that winter of 1819, while tending his traps and gathering his pelts along the Mississippi River, he dreamed of her pale, luminous skin, her shining hair, and the bell-like music of her laughter. Came spring and the Indian chief presented himself at the trading post with a splendid bounty of beaver and fox as payment for her hand in marriage.

The young woman was at first stunned—and then she became scornful as the love-struck Algonquin made his proposal. "Marry you?" she laughed mockingly. "Do you think I would come live with you in some wigwam in the woods—like a squaw?"

The uncomprehending chief persisted. He proudly offered his best ponies as well as his finest furs. The Frenchwoman became incensed at the Indian's presumption. By now, her brother had arrived on the scene and a crowd was gathering. The situation grew ugly.

In the face of the menacing mob, the Algonquin's surprise turned to embarrassment, apprehension, then anger. He leaped on his horse and wheeled the animal around.

"May the filthy spot on which your church stands be destroyed!" he shouted. "May your homes and farms be ruined, may your dead be torn from their graves, and may your land be a feeding place for fishes!"

Someone threw a rock. It struck the Indian on the forehead. He reeled from the blow but managed to stay on his horse. Whirling again, he spat furiously on the ground and, with blood streaming from his wound, galloped out of the village.

The rejected chief never returned to Kaskaskia, and the villagers laughed off his malediction. It is doubtful that either the chief or any of those confronting him on that day in 1819 remained alive sixty-two years later, when the curse of the Algonquin came true. In 1881, the Mississippi overflowed its banks, inundating the village in the worst flood of the century. The raging waters destroyed Kaskaskia's Church of the Immaculate Conception, swept away the farmers' crops, and washed out the local cemetery, scooping up the dead and floating them downriver in their wooden coffins. Nearly every house was destroyed. The current cut a new channel, leaving the site of the village permanently underwater. As the muddy river flowed over what had once been a thriving community, it is possible that some Kaskaskians remembered hearing of the Indian chief's curse, for their town had truly become a "feeding place for fishes."

A calamitous coincidence? Perhaps. And yet there are many students of the occult who consider the disaster in Kaskaskia dramatic proof of the Indian's magical powers. Whether or not the chief's malediction had any real effect, such an idiosyncratic attempt to circumvent the laws of nature falls within the province of low magic—a craft that is older than recorded history. This type of magic has found root in the beliefs of virtually every society down through the ages. In contrast to the complex ceremonial arts practiced by high priests, such as Jo-

hann Faust and the Count Cagliostro, low magic is invoked to secure some particular personal advantage—to gain wealth, to succeed in love or in any number of other pursuits, or to exact retribution for some insult or harm.

Such folk magic can be as simple as the hurling of a curse and the casting of a spell—or as elaborate as a quasi-religious ceremony, with costumes, music, and prayerlike incantations. It can involve all manner of charms and talismans and include potions of fantastic ingredients and astounding diversity. It can manifest apparent results with terrifying speed, or work with an exquisite and implacable slowness. Its practitioners may be anyone seemingly endowed with magical powers, private individuals or professional witches and medicine men.

The Algonquin's malison on Kaskaskia was far from an isolated occurrence among the first Americans. Indians across the land made broad use of magic, and shamans wielded enormous influence throughout the tribes. Among the Navajo of the Southwest, ancient tradition held that *chindi,* or evil spirits, could be invoked to call down frightful curses on enemies. A remarkable story dating from 1825 describes the demise of a powerful clan named Long Salt that had run afoul of a blind old medicine man. The family had engaged the medicine man to exorcise the vengeful spirit of a slain enemy—but then had been unwise enough to cheat the sightless shaman by paying him in wild antelope meat instead of the promised and more valuable mutton.

Before long, members of the family, some old and feeble, some young and in robust health, began dying for no apparent reason. Every few weeks, a Long Salt would falter and die. It soon became obvious to the clan's headmen that someone had set a chindi on them. A delegation sought out the shaman and confessed their foolish sin—and he in turn advised that he had instructed the chindi to annihilate the Long Salts for their wickedness. After much beseeching, the aged shaman finally relented; he told the Long Salts to return in ten days, at which time he would name his price for absolution.

But when the Long Salts appeared on the appointed day, they found to their dismay that the old medicine man had passed away—and they had no idea whether or not he had removed the chindi. The answer seemed apparent upon their return home; several newly stricken members of the family lay dying. Over the generations, the Long Salts steadily declined; by 1900, only 10 remained of a clan that once numbered more than 100. In the winter of 1928, the last of the Long Salts, a woman named Alice, died of a malady that defied the medical science of the day. The vengeance of the chindi was perfect.

Modern researchers might attribute the end of the Long Salts to a genetic disorder or to some rare and then unknown disease. Whatever the case, the Long Salts fervently believed in the powers of the shaman and of the chindi; they despaired, feeling themselves doomed. And that by itself may have been magic enough.

Among Native Americans, the magician's powers were thought to derive in part from a special ability to commune with the spirit world through visions. To achieve a vision, a medicine man might fast or take long sweat baths or even indulge in ritualized self-torture. Such was the case for participants in the Sun Dance, a ceremony practiced by the Plains Indians during their bitter struggles with the U.S. Army in the latter half of the nineteenth century.

A warrior undertaking the Sun Dance endured unbelievable pain in order to gain an advantage over his foes. First his chest muscles were pierced by sharpened sticks. Thongs slung from a pole were then tied to the sticks and tightened, lifting the participant off the ground and forcing him to dance on his tiptoes. Prior to the battle of Little Bighorn in 1876, the great Sioux leader Sitting Bull danced for two days in this torturous manner. At last the man collapsed, falling into a trance in which he dreamed of Indians massacring soldiers, whose bodies fell like rain from the sky.

To the Sioux, Sitting Bull's dream was a prophecy from on high, powerful medicine that would assure the enemy's defeat. To further strengthen their prowess, the Sioux warriors

Inside a sun lodge early in the twentieth century, Blackfoot elders blow eagle-bone whistles to bring good weather for the four to eight days of the Sun Dance. By solemnizing their ties to nature, the tribe hoped to ensure a year of health and abundance.

arranged various objects in symbolic ways. Three red stones placed in a row represented victory. Two buffalo skulls, one that of a bull, the other of a cow, were set on a cairn with a stick pointing from the bull's skull to the cow's—meaning that the Sioux would fight like bulls, while the American soldiers would run like women.

When warriors and soldiers met on the Little Bighorn River several days later, Lt. Col. George A. Custer and 225 men of the Seventh Cavalry were annihilated in the Plains Indians' greatest victory against their white enemies. The five-to-one superiority in numbers enjoyed by the Sioux and their Cheyenne allies undoubtedly was a factor, but who could say that the power of Sitting Bull's vision and the magic of the rocks and skulls—as well as the confidence that they instilled—did not also affect the outcome?

In the days when they engaged in tribal warfare and headhunting, the fierce Aguaruna of the upper Amazon would not consider going into battle without first dreaming of their foes. By fasting and chewing the leaves of mind-altering plants, an Aguaruna could experience an intense vision in which the spirit of a departed warrior—known as an *ajútap*—appeared, describing in elaborate detail the dreamer's future triumphs in battle. In the language of the Aguaruna, the dreamer became a *kajintin,* or "dream owner." According to tradition, the dream of a slain kajintin left his body on the very night of his death and was trans-

In voodoo lore, a gris-gris bag draws power from its contents—here, including nail parings, roots, leaves, and hair.

formed into an ajútap that would visit other warriors in their visions.

Objects, too, played—and still play—a vital role in Aguaruna magic. Hunters aver that certain stones, known as *yuka,* have an affinity for various kinds of birds and animals. Carrying the stones will help to attract game and ensure success in the hunt. Other stones called *nantag* are believed to increase the productivity of crops—red pebbles for manioc, black for yams—and are a woman's most prized possessions; she keeps them securely wrapped and well nourished with herbal water. Otherwise they might decide to run away.

Such "medicine bags," holding sacred stones and other magical objects, are an important part of the folk tradition in many lands. Practitioners of voodoo, the magic brought to the New World centuries ago by slaves from Africa, have long relied on similar charms to bring good luck or to ward off bad. And while voodoo has declined since its heyday in the 1800s, it is still a factor in the life of certain New Orleans neighborhoods and Louisiana parishes, and it remains powerful in the villages and towns of Haiti.

In Louisiana and Haiti, the voodoo pouches are called gris-gris, French for "gray-gray," because more often than not they are used for both benign white and malignant black magic. The things that go into a gris-gris can range from the mundane to the bizarre and may include fingernail clippings or a bit of sweat-stained clothing from the owner, dirt from a graveyard, bone fragments, dried herbs, rock salt, or alligator teeth.

The bag holding the gris-gris is often sewn from red flannel (red being supposed a favorite color of spirits), although other materials may be used. If the gris-gris's purpose is to increase the sexual prowess of its owner, the bag may be fashioned from the scrotum of a goat. William Seabrook, a writer who lived in Haiti during the 1920s, described how an old voodoo priestess named Maman Célie made such a love charm to ensure her grandson's success in winning a girl who had theretofore shunned him. She first ground up the dried body of a hummingbird in a wooden cup, then added some jungle-flower pollen and some drops of her grandson's blood and semen, all the while uttering an incomprehensible chant. According to Seabrook, the grandson threw Maman Célie's bizarre concoction full into the girl's face as she passed him the following Saturday evening, and within a few hours she had yielded to his advances.

In New Orleans, the most famous of all the voodoo queens was a woman named Marie Laveau. Actually, there were two women named Marie Laveau, a mother and daughter who between them plied their occult trade through most of the nineteenth century. Many of the Laveau clients sought help in affairs of the heart, and the Laveau ladies were never short of prescriptions. A favorite wile for a woman in love was to steal a glove from the man she was after, then fill it with sugar and honey to sweeten his affection and with steel dust to

As old New Orleans's reigning voodoo queen, Marie Laveau the elder attained wealth and social standing.

strengthen her power over the intended; to make it all work, the lady had only to sleep with the glove under her mattress. A woman worried about a straying husband might mix a few drops of her menstrual blood with his dinner. Women who had applied this curative to their men often referred to it as the Marie Laveau trick.

If a woman passionately desired a married man, Marie would write the names of the man and his wife on a piece of paper and place it in an animal's bladder, then hang the bladder in the sun to dry. The man, it was said, would leave his wife, and all his new flame had to do to keep him was to apply sufficient love powders and oils—also provided by Marie. Conversely, for parents who disapproved of the man courting their daughter, Marie would mix a favorite gris-gris, whose ingredients included gunpowder, dried mud from a wasp's nest, flaxseed, cayenne pepper, shotgun pellets, powdered sassafras, bluestone, and dragon's blood—the whole thing to be tossed on the steps of the undesirable suitor's house. Presumably, the young man would get the message, before even more powerful magic was applied.

There was all manner of gris-gris available for virtually every situation—to assure gamblers of winning, to make misers part with their cash, to cure snakebites, to win court cases, to help preachers stay in the good graces of their congregations—although these same preachers would sometimes denounce the voodoo queens from their pulpits. And there were numerous ways of dealing with enemies. Special "conjure balls" could be purchased at the Laveau cottage. These were constructed out of black wax and were supposed to contain a piece of human flesh; often they were pierced by pins or smeared with blood. The voodoo queens instructed their customers to roll the balls across an enemy's lawn, after which death or misfortune would befall the owners.

Although voodoo was mainly a folk magic for the descendants of African slaves, more than a few affluent New Orleans whites became clients of the two Maries—and a number of others were subjected to their magic. For a price, the Laveau women would teach the preparation of certain gris-gris, and it was not unusual for mistresses unpopular with their servants to find that their bed pillows had become exceedingly uncomfortable—not to mention somewhat horrifying. The pillow might contain hard clumps of feathers tied in the shape of roosters or pecans pierced with a pair of crossed feathers. A particularly evil gris-gris aimed at offensive whites consisted of saffron, salt, gunpowder, and ground-up dog droppings, all neatly folded into a black paper sack. The gris-gris was placed in some part of the house, such as a cabinet or a dresser drawer, where the intended victim would eventually find it. Sometimes a servant secreted it in her master's jacket pocket; and more than one society debutante was shocked, in the midst of a ball or some other grand occasion, to come upon such an item in her handbag.

Gris-gris was but one of many kinds of symbolic objects important to voodoo, then and now. Indeed, the very name *voodoo* probably derives from a word in the Dahomey language of West Africa meaning fetish, which within the context of African voodoo means an object in the physical world embodying a spirit. Talismans—designs carved in wood or drawn on parchment using the blood of a human or a dove—are worn as necklaces to attract friendly spirits. Amulets such as birthstones or shells have a similar purpose. A *ju-ju* is a grotesque wooden carving or the skull of an animal such as a horse, alligator, cow, or goat, painted with crosses and oth-

er occult markings; hung from the wall of a house, it is believed to ward off evil spirits. A *vever*—an elaborate pattern fraught with symbols painted on the floor of a house—attracts beneficent spirits.

Voodoo cultists also hang special lamps, often made from the shells of coconuts and fueled with a mixture of oil and various other ingredients. The oil of a charm lamp—meant to attract the love of a particular person—contains sugar, honey, perfume, and flower petals, as well as bits of a sheep's brain. The mixture burned in a so-called black lamp—usually hung outdoors and used for such negative purposes as driving an enemy from the neighborhood or making someone ill—can include soot and ground pepper, along with a powder concocted out of dried lizard and a decomposed corpse.

One dread form of African-Haitian magic involves dressing a corpse in clothes belonging to the person who has been marked for revenge, then leaving it to rot in a secret hideaway. For those who believe in voodoo, the effect can be devastating. Upon learning of this hidden horror, men have gone mad or died from fatigue, thirst, and hunger in their desperate search to uncover the corpse and thus break the spell.

Not all voodoo is concerned with the laying on or warding off of curses. In Haiti, where voodoo is practiced as high magic as well as low, it assumes many of the trappings of a formal religion—one that is still close to its West African roots but infused with elements of Roman Catholicism. Voodoo priests and priestesses—known as *houngans* and *mambos*—wear vestments derived from those of the Catholic clergy. Voodoo has a calendar for special ceremonies to be performed throughout the year that is similar to the Christian calendar of holy days. Ritual baths recall Christian baptism and may be taken during major Christian festivals such as Christmas, when throngs of chanting bathers wade into the ocean, each carrying exactly seven, ten, or twenty-one slices of lime, these numbers possessing certain magical qualities.

Students of voodoo believe that the cult has also been

influenced by the Carib and Arawak Indians, both now almost extinct, who populated Hispaniola when the Spaniards first arrived there in the 1490s. Voodoo chants use words that cannot be traced to French, Spanish, or any West African tongue but may have originated from Carib or other early Indian languages.

Despite some borrowings from Christianity, voodoo as practiced in Haiti remains a sort of pagan pantheism, in which hundreds of different gods or spirits, known as *loas,* may be invoked in rites such as the *petro* (the name derives from a voodoo priest, a certain Don Pedro, with whom it was originally associated). One important loa is Damballah, the serpent god, whose presence is sometimes symbolized by a painting or a carving of a snake kept near the altar.

A petro can be an elaborate affair or-chestrated by a houngan, a mambo, and many assistants and carried out according to a relatively predictable sequence, starting with a ritual libation—usually water—the invocations of loas, the drawing of vevers on the floor, as well as prayers and chants. Communicants may then make food offerings to a loa, placing a few ears of corn or some grain or fruit on the vever appropriate to that loa.

Music and dance are essential in the petro, with the rhythm of drums, bells, and rattles growing in volume and intensity as the ceremony progresses. Rites commonly last from dusk to dawn and may even extend for several days. Often the culmination is the sacrifice of an animal—usually a chicken, but sometimes a goat, a pig, or a bull. For anyone who participates in the petro, the goal is to become more and more closely attuned to the loa being invoked. A few even seem to become possessed—they are carried away by their ecstatic frame of mind, convinced that the spirit has entered their bodies.

The most lurid voodoo traditions are those surrounding zombies. In Haitian tradition, zombies are the "living dead," corpses resurrected from the grave and brought by voodoo magic to a robotic semblance of life, after which they become slaves. The folklore is replete with grim—if largely unsubstantiated—tales of zombies. Researcher William Seabrook reports hearing of a gang of zombies who worked in a cane field under an especially cruel master. One day when the master was gone, the woman placed in charge of the zombies—a kindlier sort—decided to give them a treat and took them to the local market. The zombies' relatives were horrified to see their dead kin walking blank-eyed among them. But the zombies were not totally unaware. Returning to the fields, they passed the cemetery where they had been buried and immediately rushed into it, clawing the earth in a pathetic attempt to return to their graves.

Later, after a Haitian friend introduced him to a supposed zombie, Seabrook concluded that it was all a hoax—that the zombie in fact was a living, breathing human being, though severely retarded.

Seabrook was partly right. He subsequently uncovered an additional clue as to the actual nature of so-called zombies. It was buried in the Haitian penal code, which forbids the administration of any substance capable of inducing a prolonged coma. The law specifies that a person drugging anyone in this manner can be charged with murder if he or she buries the victim—even if the victim manages to survive the ordeal.

The law derives from an old voodoo practice that is believed by some to persist in Haiti to this day (see page 88). A victim who has been marked by a houngan or mambo to become a zombie is drugged with a special potion made from the organs of a poisonous blowfish and certain alkaline roots. The drug slows the person's heartbeat and renders him comatose. Under the direction of the priest, he is then placed in a coffin, buried in the morning, and removed from the grave the following night. When the victim is disinterred, the priest administers an antidote to neutralize the poison and restore a normal heartbeat. According to some accounts, however, the victim's brain, by this time, has been so deprived of oxygen that his higher intellectual faculties are greatly diminished and he is left in a permanent trancelike state.

As part of this macabre ceremony, the zombie is reportedly given a small black coffin to hold while he dances around in a frenzy, until dropping from exhaustion. Tradition maintains that because a zombie has come back from the grave, he can then be of use in communicating with the spirits of the dead.

In Hawaii, a magical folk religion somewhat akin to voodoo held sway over the spiritual life of the native islanders until well into the nineteenth century, and traces of the tradition persist to this day. The religion had its origins among the Hawaiians' forebears, the great Polynesian navigators who carried their beliefs with them when they first settled the islands around AD 750. In the fertile soil of Hawaii, the religion prospered and developed the greatest variety of priestly orders among any of the dozen or so Polynesian tribes scattered across the Pacific.

Chief among these priests were the sorcerers known as kahunas, who were avowed to possess fabulous powers, which like most folk magic could be employed for either good or evil purposes. "Killing" priests—those who used their magic to exact revenge or for some other dark gain—were known as kahuna ana'anas. They specialized in curses that allegedly could cause a victim to grow weak and die within days. A person who was bent on revenge could hire the services of a killing priest and his spiritual assistant, known as an unihipili. This was a special spirit that owed sole allegiance to its particular kahuna. Ideally, a kahuna's unihipili would be the spirit of a kinsman who had died in infancy, and thus could be trusted implicitly. But an unihipili could behave in unpredictable ways and, if it was not well treated, might even turn on its master. A wise kahuna went to great lengths to ensure that his unihipili was well fed and contented. At every meal, the kahuna said prayers for his unihipili and fed it by dipping his fingers into a bowl of awa (the juice of a medicinal root) and flicking drops of the substance into the air.

The foundation of the kahuna's power was the belief

among native Hawaiians that everyone is endowed with two spirits and that when a person goes to sleep, one spirit is left in charge while the other wanders freely, giving rise to dreams. In cases of revenge, the job of the unihipili was to lure the roving spirit of the intended victim into the clutches of the kahuna ana'ana.

Usually, this task was accomplished by sending the unihipili out into the night to collect other wandering spirits for a gala at the home of its master. Joining in the party was the unsuspecting spirit of the victim. At the proper moment, the kahuna ana'ana would offer the fated spirit a bowl of awa. The instant the spirit touched its lips to the bowl, the kahuna ana'ana would seize his prey and crush it in his two hands. The spirit would vanish, leaving behind a single drop of blood, which the kahuna ana'ana would mix with poi and eat. The next day, the victim would be told how his spirit had been captured and slain by the great kahuna ana'ana. According to Hawaiian tradition, the victim's will to live was completely destroyed in this manner, and within a day or two he would perish.

Many Hawaiians also believed that some people were afflicted with errant spirits that simply might not return when the flesh-and-blood individuals awoke. If that happened, it was thought that the person would fall into a deathlike trance and would remain insensible until the spirit returned. This predicament required the services of a kahuna, who upon recapturing the spirit, would endeavor to force it back into the body through a raised toenail—never through the mouth, from which it might escape again.

A kahuna ana'ana, it was understood, also had the ability to "pray" someone into oblivion. In the ritual surrounding a death prayer, the priest concocted a special stew that included either pork or the meat from a dog that had been fattened on poi and coconut milk. To the cooking fire he added some article that belonged to the victim toward whom the prayer was being directed—a lock of hair, a fingernail clipping, a fragment of clothing. The priest and his client then ate the stew while praying for the demise of the client's enemy.

The next morning, as in the crushing of a spirit, the kahuna ana'ana made sure that the victim learned what had transpired during the night. The terrible knowledge that he was the object of a death prayer was apparently all that was needed to send the victim to his grave. The first dread sign that the curse was working would be a tingling in the feet, followed by numbness. The numbness would turn to paralysis, which would work its way up the legs to the torso. The victim was by then certain that a ravenous unihipili was consuming his vital energy, or mana. Eventually, he would succumb.

Death prayers were usually directed by native Hawaiians against others of their kind. But on occasion, the wrath of the priests was leveled at whites, or haoles, some of whom died under circumstances that Hawaiians attributed to the magic of a kahuna ana'ana.

Throughout most of the nineteenth century, Hawaii was an independent land ruled by a royal family. In 1893, a coup led by Americans, Britons, and Germans overthrew the reigning queen and opened the way for the United States to annex the Hawaiian Islands a few years later. The resident Americans and Britons supporting the coup and agitating for annexation were detested by those Hawaiians who saw the end of royal rule as conquest by the haoles. All over the islands, kahuna ana'anas began uttering death prayers against American and British officials and their families. On the very day of the coup, Anne Stevens, the daughter of the ardently annexationist former U.S. minister to Hawaii, died of drowning. "Our prayers have begun to work," chanted the sorcerers. "Our work is preordained." Just two years later, Stevens himself died at his stateside home in Maine.

Other deaths occurred within a few years among prominent supporters of American Manifest Destiny in Hawaii: Henry N. Castle, an immensely wealthy planter and publisher, died with his small daughter when the German liner *Elbe* was rammed and sunk; Navy captain Gilbert

A Haitian voodoo priest conse-crates an intricate design called a vever, which symbolizes the presence of a loa, or deity. Traced in cornmeal, the vever is a place for celebrating magical rites. Here, the priest offers sugar and rum to entice the loa to partake of his ceremony.

Among the most en-during was the idea that spirits of both the dead and the living haunt the islands. According to this view, when a per-son died, his spirit left the body via the mouth or nostrils. The spirit's new "home" was the grave of the deceased, from which it ventured forth at night to create all manner of mis-chief. A wayward spirit could become a special nuisance to members of the deceased's family, who frequently found them-

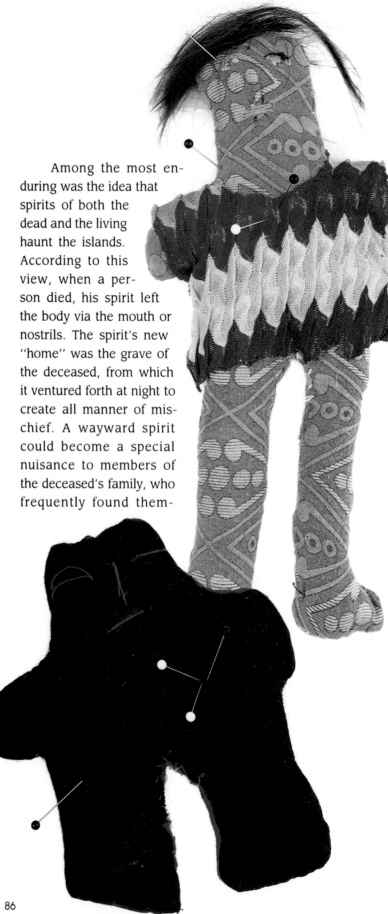

Wiltse, who enraged Hawai-ians by declaring, "We will make an American lake of the Pacific," was stricken by a massive brain clot; Albert S. Willis, U.S. minister to Ha-waii, who although a sup-porter of Hawaiian independence, was after all an impor-tant haole, perished of tuberculosis; Colonel A. G. S. Hawes, the British consul general who offered an immense floral tribute at Willis's funeral, died shortly thereafter of com-plications brought on by a carbuncle on his neck. Al-though Westerners might shrug off any connection with ancient Hawaiian death prayers, many islanders remained convinced that their kahuna ana'anas had precipitated the fatal accidents and illnesses.

It has been said that with the possible exceptions of the Chinese, the Irish, and the New Zealand Maori, the early Hawaiians were among the most superstitious people on earth. True or not, it is certain that the islanders entertained a mass of magical beliefs that went far beyond the ministra-tions of the kahuna ana'anas.

selves the butt of its practical jokes. Some spirits were incorrigibly juvenile—tripping people, showering them with pebbles, tweaking them in their sleep, or emitting strange twittering sounds or unpleasant odors in their presence. Families took elaborate measures to keep troublesome spirits in their place. Covering a grave with thorns and animal droppings was thought to provide some protection, but many families went one step further by constructing stone barriers over the graves of their kin.

The interaction of spirit and body was the foundation of Hawaiian folk medicine. A special caste of healing kahunas, known as the *kahuna la'au lapa'au,* practiced a kind of holistic medicine based on the effect of what Westerners would call the mind on the body. In the view of a kahuna la'au lapa'au, a person's mind or spiritual self was made up of several parts. The most important of these was the *kane,* or higher self. The kane was the individual's source of mana and in Judeo-Christian terms was roughly analogous to the soul. The body itself—known as the *kino*—was a physical expression of the kane. Whether a person was healthy or sick was determined by how closely kane and kino were in harmony—something akin to the yin and the yang of Chinese tradition.

Several intermediary states were involved in the kane-

Voodoo dolls like these are thought to impart control over people for good or evil purposes. A doll can be made of fabric, wax, wood, or clay and stuffed with moss or herbs. It must contain something of the person it is meant to control, typically nail clippings, hair, or photographs. The magic is activated by pricking the effigy—white needles if the intent is to heal, black to hex.

87

A Pharmacological Theory about Zombies

A Haitian identified as Clairvius Narcisse believes he was a zombie—one of the living dead—and a number of scientists think he is right. Narcisse was pronounced dead in 1962 at a hospital in Haiti. A death certificate was issued, and Narcisse was buried. But in 1980, a man saying he was Clairvius Narcisse told a chilling tale.

The man said he had remained conscious even when his body lost all signs of life. Three days after his burial, he was disinterred, bound, and enslaved in a plantation in northern Haiti. His captor was a malevolent sorcerer called a *bokor*. Narcisse escaped but did not return home until the death of his brother, whom he blamed for his enslavement. Family members agreed he was indeed the relative they had thought dead.

Wade Davis, a Harvard-trained scientist who studied the man's claims, investigated poisons that might induce a deathlike state. He found that so-called zombie powders almost always included ground-up puffer fish, whose organs harbor a poison called tetrodotoxin.

Victims of tetrodotoxin-poisoning experience total paralysis and very light breathing; survivors report being fully conscious but unable to respond to their surroundings. If Narcisse was dosed with such a poison, he might have appeared dead even to his doctors and might have remained paralyzed until after his burial. Only the bokor and Narcisse would have known the truth. Davis's theory has encountered skepticism in the United States but has yet to be definitively proved or dismissed.

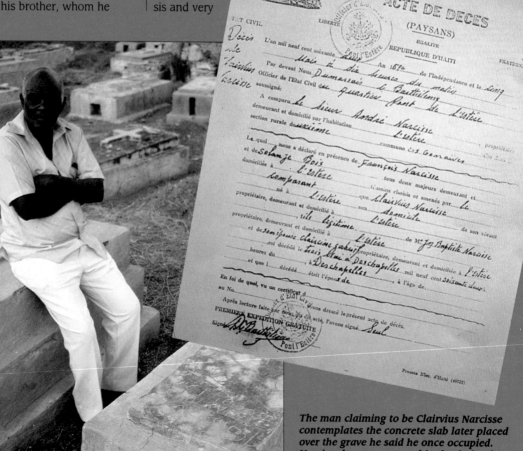

The man claiming to be Clairvius Narcisse contemplates the concrete slab later placed over the grave he said he once occupied. Narcisse bears a scar on his cheek that he claims was caused by a nail driven through his coffin. The 1962 death certificate (above) bears the thumbprint of Narcisse's sister Marie Claire, who identified his body.

Cotton nose plugs, a broad-brimmed hat, and a burlap bag protect a voodoo chemist from the harmful properties of the powders he prepares. He works under the guidance of a bokor, who is responsible for the efficacy of the drug but has no actual contact with the poisons.

Human bones—here being ground to dust—are vital components of zombie powders according to Haitian occult tradition. One such powder included bones, puffer fish, freshly killed lizards, the dried carcass of a toad with poisonous glands, and two extremely toxic plants. In a laboratory test commissioned by Wade Davis as part of his study on zombiism, the powder rendered animals comatose for twenty-four hours but did not leave any discernible permanent injuries.

kino connection. The *aka* was a kind of template or blueprint of the kane. The *ku* regulated the kino, overseeing and controlling all bodily functions. Using the aka as its guide, the ku sought to keep the kino matched as closely as possible with the kane. Problems arose when disease or injury intruded on the body through the *lono,* the part of the spiritual self concerned with the outside physical world. In the treatment of disease or injury, the kahuna la'au lapa'au's magic worked indirectly. An injury such as a broken bone, for example, was replicated in the aka. To heal the break, the kahuna directed mana from the kane to the injured part of the aka, restoring the latter to its original idealized state. Then the restored part of aka was transferred to the kino, thus healing the broken bone.

The kane-kino connection was so central to the beliefs of the Hawaiian folk healers that, before administering treatment, a kahuna la'au lapa'au made certain that the patient was in the right mental state to receive it. The kahuna might even decline to give treatment if the patient lacked a disposition that the healer deemed favorable to recovery. To determine this, the kahuna looked for signs in the patient's dreams. Those dreams auguring a recovery might contain any of a wide variety of seemingly unrelated images: canoes, blood-red rain, strange cloud formations, rainbows, and excrement. In especially difficult cases, several kahuna la'au lapa'aus might work together like a team of physicians—one kahuna calling good spirits, another exorcising evil ones, a third administering herbal medicines, and a fourth propitiating the gods with offerings of meat or vegetables.

Priests who specialized in the wounds sustained in battle were in great demand among the Hawaiian nobility. Generals placed their kahuna la'au lapa'aus directly behind the battle lines. Another specialist included in every royal entourage was a priest versed in the cures for the poisons common to court intrigues.

With the coming of the Christian missionaries, who were working assiduously to eradicate the old beliefs, the kahunas went into gradual decline. By the 1920s and 1930s, scarcely any of the priests, either the death-praying kahuna ana'anas or the healing kahuna la'au lapa'aus, were thought to remain in practice. But old ways die hard, and from time to time, there are reports of holdovers still practicing their arts.

The kahuna la'au lapa'aus, in particular, seem to be surviving in small numbers on every island. Researcher Julius Scammon Rodman, whose investigations of Hawaiian folk magic span nearly half a century, records that he personally has seen kahunas heal hideous gangrenous wounds that had festered for months and that had failed to respond to conventional treatment. Rodman also reports a case in the 1950s of a native Hawaiian boy brought to Honolulu's Queens Hospital with a broken back. According to the researcher, the lad was assumed to be permanently paralyzed when x-rays showed that his spinal cord had been severed. But the doctors acquiesced when the boy's mother insisted on calling in a kahuna la'au lapa'au, and they were astounded when this "healing" priest performed the medical miracle of inducing the boy's spinal cord to knit back together—as further x-rays proved. Somehow, writes Rodman, "the kahuna knew the secret of taking over control of the patient's autonomic nervous system and issuing messages over its network, directing a super speedup of the healing forces at work on the lesion."

Although many Westerners are inclined to turn a blind eye toward anything in their own heritage that smacks of superstition, European culture has a strong folk-magic tradition of its own. Behind the facade of conventional Christianity, medieval Europe bubbled with bizarre beliefs about the power of spells, charms, and potions. Like Haitian voodoo, medieval black magic sometimes adopted parts of the Catholic liturgy. One prescription for harming an enemy instructed the zealot to dig up a coffin and remove its nails, while uttering, "I take you so you may serve to cause evil to all persons whom I will—in the name of the Father, the Son, and the Holy Spirit, amen." Next, the spellbinder had to find

When this photo was taken in the 1890s, Daniel Hookala was thought to be one of the last practitioners of Hawaiian kahuna magic. Hookala, a healer specializing in herbal cures, died in 1939 at the age of 103, but kahuna magic has since been revived by others.

a footprint of his enemy and drive one or more of the coffin nails into it, while intoning a perversion of the Lord's Prayer: "Our Father, who art on earth. . . ." At the same time, he invoked the name of the person on whom the spell was to be cast.

The grisliest object in medieval black magic was the so-called hand of glory. This was the amputated and preserved hand of a hanged man, a relic whose sole purpose seems to have been to enable the user to burglarize other people's houses *(page 104)*. But spells and potions to help in love or sex were also mainstays of the medieval magician's art. One stratagem for the love-struck man was to write three times on the back of a mirror the name of the woman he desired, hold the mirror up to a pair of copulating dogs, and then hide the mirror for nine days at a spot near where the woman passed. The mirror would magically connect the woman, the sex act, and her would-be lover, who by carrying the mirror on his person thereafter possessed the power to seduce her.

Medieval women sometimes gave a vulgar twist to the idea that the way to a man's heart is through his stomach. A maid, it was widely believed, might win a man by feeding him the products of her body. In making a lover's pie, she was advised to perspire profusely by taking a very hot bath, then to cover herself with flour to absorb the perspiration. Next, she was to wipe off the flour into a baking dish and to the flour add a powder made of burnt hairs from different parts of her body, along with clippings from her toenails and fingernails. A beaten egg would go in for binding, after which the whole would be baked and served to the man of the lady's choice.

Love magic could occasionally backfire, as any Elizabethan admirer of Shakespeare could attest. The comedic plot of *A Midsummer Night's Dream* revolves around love charms that go awry when one character falls in love with another who has been transformed by a fairy queen and has the head of an ass. And sixteenth-century Scots chuckled over the story of a school-

teacher who was smitten by the sister of one of his pupils. The teacher persuaded the pupil to steal into his sister's room while she slept and to pluck for him some of her pubic hairs. The teacher intended to make use of the hairs in casting a spell that would render the girl in his power. Unfortunately, the boy botched the job; his sister awoke and let out a scream. After the boy confessed, his mother substituted three hairs from a cow's udder. The boy dutifully passed these on to the teacher, who according to a contemporary account, ''wrought his art upon them.'' Only later did he discover that it was the heifer that fell under his charm, following him through the town with lovesick moos.

Animal parts were often key ingredients in lovers' spells and potions. The *Grimorium Verum*, a medieval text on magic, prescribed a procedure for getting a girl to dance naked by writing the magic word *frutimiere* on parchment, using ink made from the blood of a bat. If the parchment was placed under a door through which the girl passed, she would fall under its spell and automatically enter the nearest room, strip off all of her clothes, and dance in frenzied abandon. The *Grimorium* cautioned, however, that ''her grimaces and contortions will cause more pity than desire.''

According to medieval tradition, a husband suspecting his wife of infidelity

A Gallery of Demons

Within the human mind, demons have a long and rich history. Just as benevolent spirits were worshiped as the source of good, demons were blamed for the world's evils. People assigned names, forms, and functions to demons. And since misfortune was never very far from one's door, the evil legions multiplied as eons passed.

By the Middle Ages, the air of Christian Europe was thick with fiends. "Several demons pursue each human being," reported one thirteenth-century abbot. "Just as a man who plunged into the sea is wholly surrounded by water, above and below, so demons, too, flow around a man from all sides." In a breathtaking display of exactitude, this cleric declared that 1,758,176 demons beset the world. Three centuries later, scholars put the number at 7,405,926.

Demonologists compiled vast catalogs listing the names, ranks, and specialties of the hellish host—from Satan, who led the forces of darkness, to Ukobach, who stoked the furnaces of hell. The tomes detailed which demons could induce or cure disease, direct the course of love, or control the weather.

A skilled magician was thought to be able to traffic with the evil beings. Some people believe that a sorcerer with the correct spells can summon up a fiend and order it to perform a specific task. The first step is to find the right demon for the job by consulting a book of demonology. The names and personalities of demons differ from place to place; the sampling on these pages is from Collin de Plancy's 1863 *Dictionnaire Infernal*.

Eurynome

A magician intent on murder might invoke Eurynome, the prince of death, whose body is covered with oozing sores and who dines on decaying flesh.

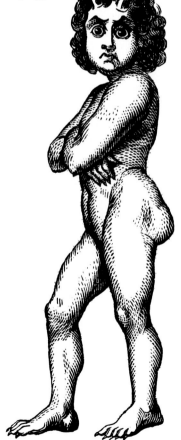

Beelzebub

One of many different names and guises attributed to Satan is Beelzebub, here depicted in accordance with the name's meaning—"Lord of Flies."

Lucifer

Lucifer, another of Satan's alter egos, appears as a sullen child—fittingly, since his rebellious attitude toward God led to his being cast from heaven.

Behemoth

Patron of gluttony and greed, Behemoth (right) serves as hell's wine steward. He may take the form of a variety of large animals, including an elephant, and his stolid tread is said to cause earthquakes.

Leonard

A triple-horned demon with fox's ears (above), Leonard is the inspector general of sorcery and black magic and sits as the grand master of the witches' sabbat. Despite his powerful offices and commanding presence—he may also take the form of a greyhound or a bull— Leonard is said to be taciturn and melancholy.

Belphegor

This sluggish-looking fiend, who is sometimes depicted as a young girl, has been dubbed the demon of sloth. Lazy sorcerers apparently appeal to Belphegor to provide them with easy wealth or the ability to invent laborsaving devices.

Stolas

A wise owl of a devil who commands twenty-six demonic legions, Stolas can teach adepts the secrets of astronomy as well as the properties of various plants and precious gems.

Cerberus

Cerberus (above), whose origins are found in Greek mythology, is credited with granting eloquence to the tongue-tied. But would-be orators, be wary— the bite of this dog-headed demon brings instant death.

Malphas

This hardworking builder-demon can be summoned to construct impregnable fortresses and to help breach an enemy's ramparts. Malphas also seeks out good laborers.

Flauros

With eyes of fire, catlike Flauros is said to see the past, present, and future. He commands twenty Satanic legions and can rouse the entire demon army against an enemy.

Furfur

Some say Furfur, a flying stag with razor-sharp claws, can summon thunder and lightning at will. A mercurial demon, he can also be called upon to maintain domestic harmony.

Caacrinolas

A kind of dog-headed griffin, Caacrinolas (above) is said to predict the future. He can also render humans invisible and incite them to murder.

Ronwe

A marquis in the demon hierarchy, Ronwe (below) reportedly can grant fluency in any language. He also can make the most unpleasant magician— even, presumably, one who picks his nose—beloved by all.

Buer

This multilimbed fiend, who moves by rolling like a wheel, supposedly instructs his summoners in philosophy and logic. Buer also provides good servants and cures the ill.

Adramelech

Believed to be lord chancellor of hell and steward of Satan's private council, Adramelech displays pride in his position—and perhaps a stubborn streak—by taking the form of a mule with peacock feathers.

Ukobach

Ukobach, an imp counted in the lowest order of demons, supplies oil to hell's furnaces and sometimes appears with his body in flames. This demon is credited with inventing fireworks as well as fried food.

Ribesal

This odd-looking fiend, whose appendages represent a variety of creatures, is another lowly demon. Ribesal nevertheless is responsible for such tasks as raising tempests and blanketing mountains with snow.

could get her to reveal her most intimate secrets by placing a toad's tongue on her breast while she slept. To ensure that she never coveted another man, he could burn and pulverize the ashes of a wolf's genitals, along with hair from the animal's cheeks, eyebrows, and beard. The concoction was then sprinkled in the wife's food or drink. On the other hand, a man purportedly could make himself irresistibly attractive to the woman of his dreams by serving her the dried and pulverized organs of various small creatures—a dove's heart, a sparrow's liver, a swallow's ovaries, a hare's kidney—all mixed with the would-be lover's blood.

Given what must have been the difficulty of securing such esoteric ingredients, it is not surprising that magicians often included more readily available alternatives. Plants and flowers such as lettuce, leeks, ferns, periwinkles, jasmine, crocuses, and pansies were just a few of the flora in the pharmacopoeia of medieval magicians. Some plants had actual medicinal qualities that could affect a person's behavior. Laurel could produce delirium if chewed. Poppy and nightshade could put the victim in a stupor, and early magicians knew about the stimulating properties of foxglove long before orthodox physicians began to prescribe the dried leaves of that plant for heart conditions.

Even the lowly bean had magical powers. The *Grimorium Verum* had a formula for invisibility, parts of which were grim indeed: Rise before sunrise on a Wednesday and plant seven black beans in the mouth, eyes, and ears of a corpse's severed head. Trace a pattern on the head and bury it for a week, face up and just below the surface, sprinkling the spot each morning with brandy. (It had to be good brandy, the *Grimorium* advised.) If these instructions were followed, a spirit would appear and engage the magician in the following dialogue:

Spirit: What are you doing?
Magician: Watering my plants.
Spirit: Give me the brandy—I want to water them.
Magician: Only if you can show me the pattern
I've traced on the dead man's head.

If the spirit correctly re-created the pattern, the magician knew that the spirit was beneficent, and he could allow it to water the beans. On the ninth day, according to the *Grimorium Verum,* the beans would sprout. The gardener was then to put the bean sprouts in his mouth and look into a mirror. If all had gone well, he would see no reflection of himself, for the sprouts now carried the invisibility of the dead and buried head. Under no circumstances, however, was the gardener to swallow the bean sprouts—because only by removing them from his mouth could he become visible again.

oot crops such as carrots were thought to be aphrodisiacs, probably because of their phallic shape. The mandrake root inspired a mythology all its own. A low-growing plant that thrives in the forest, the mandrake produces a thick root, often with two leglike shoots that give it a vaguely human form. The mandrake of medieval folk magic is native to Europe and goes by the scientific name of mandragora. Similar plants grow throughout temperate regions of the world and are equally steeped in folk magic. In Asia, for example, qualities similar to those possessed by the mandrake are attributed to ginseng, whose name is from the Chinese *jên-shên,* which means "man plant." Ginseng also grows in North America, along with the May apple, another common forest plant that has an anthropomorphic root. Both roots were staples in the kits of some Native American medicine men.

In fact, the mandrake root contains an alkaloid that in concentrations acts as a narcotic, and ancient magicians used it to treat everything from gout to infertility. But its human morphology, everyone agreed, made it exceedingly dangerous to handle. The ancient Greeks took elaborate precautions when digging it up. A magician was required to first draw three rings around the plant with a sword, and then face west while his apprentice danced around it, reciting erotic verse.

Medieval magicians were equally wary of the mandrake's power. They believed that the live root screamed in pain when first wrenched from the earth and that its cry could strike a person dead. To guard against this possibility, the magician stuffed his ears with candle wax, and instead of extracting the root himself, he used a dog to do the work. After loosening the dirt around the mandrake, the magician tied one end of a string around the plant and the other end to the dog. He then placed a piece of meat just out of reach of the dog and retreated a safe distance. As the dog strained to reach the meat, it pulled out the root. Legend held that the unfortunate animal almost always died upon hearing the mandrake's scream.

Magicians classified mandrake roots as male or female, depending on their species, which could be either the black or white mandragora. The white, or female, mandragora could be used to cast a love spell on a woman. The man instigating the spell took the mandrake root, spoke the woman's name over it, buried it in his garden, and fertilized it with a mix of water, milk, and his blood. On the first night of the next new moon, the man recovered the root and spent several weeks drying it and, from time to time, blessing it with incense. With the root at last properly prepared, he stuck a silver pin through its "heart" and simultaneously formed in his mind an image of the woman he desired. Left on a window sill in the full moon, the mandrake was now believed to possess magical powers that would weaken the woman's resistance.

While all this was taking place among the settled Christians of Europe, the nomadic Romany peoples were developing forms of magic that were particularly suited to their needs. Beginning about AD 1000, the Romanies wandered from India into the Middle East and Europe, where they were known as Gypsies, in the mistaken belief that they had originally come from Egypt. In their caravans and clusters of tents, the Gypsies lived close to nature, and numerous beliefs relating to animals and plants played a prominent role in their everyday lives.

A Gypsy regarded it as good luck if a bee flew into his tent. Equally promising was to catch a glimpse of a horse with its head over a gate, particularly if the horse happened to be white and if the gate had five bars. A falling star brought good luck, but the sight of a falling tree was an ill omen; Romany witches, or *chovahonni,* advised those who watched as trees were being cut to hold their ears or risk hearing the screams of the dying tree spirits. Gypsies gathered wild food such as nettles, which in their early growth could be cooked and eaten. Anyone harvesting them beyond the first of May, however, risked the ire of the devil, who was thought to collect the mature plants for use in making his shirts. Gypsy lore also blamed the devil for spoiling blackberries in the late fall—by spitting icily on them. And although it might have been tempting to collect snails for food, many Gypsies regarded that enticement as bad luck, for the snails carried their homes from place to place, just as the Gypsies did.

Being vagabonds, Gypsies relied greatly on their draft horses and went to considerable lengths to protect them from evil spirits. One way of safeguarding a horse was to sew a bit of bread or grain into the animal's collar as an antidote to black magic. To ward off the horse thieves, owners would feed a steed a piece of bread soaked with three drops of a child's blood. Sometimes more elaborate rituals were employed. In one, a Gypsy drew a ring on the horse's front left hoof and a cross on the front right hoof, all the while reciting "Stay here with me, tied by three ropes—one of God, one of the Devil, and one of Christ." Another rather obscure stratagem called for mixing clippings from the horse's mane and tail with dirt from its left fore footprint, then burying the mixture while repeating an incantation.

To protect their own health, Gypsy clans on the night of Easter Sunday passed around a box containing herbs and the dried carcass of a snake. After everyone had spit on the snake, the box and its contents were tossed into a river. This safeguard was thought to last an entire year; after that, however, it was necessary to repeat the ritual. Gypsies were wary of rats, pigs, and lizards, believing that their naked tails were signs of partnership with the devil. A rat hopping on three legs forewarned that blood would be spilled before sunset. Certain birds were also regarded as bad omens. An owl that was perched on a tent or wagon was thought to foretell ill fortune, whereas an owl heard hooting after dawn was thought to be calling the soul of a dying person. Ravens were considered to be birds of death, and a man hearing a bantam cock crowing three times could infer that someone had just cast a curse on him.

The peacock was regarded with the greatest suspicion of all, for the eye-shaped patterns on its tail feathers were seen as a sign of the devil and a graphic manifestation of the dreaded evil eye, which the Gypsies feared terribly. To guard against this curse, Gypsies wore various talismans, including blue beads and horsehair necklaces with staghorn pendants tipped with silver. Such magic jewelry was an essential part of the Gypsy wardrobe, and various types of stones were accorded different powers. Jade, onyx, and lapis lazuli sharpened the wearer's wit. Red agates, as well as amethysts and topazes, prevented headaches, while black agates imparted courage and energy. Rubies and sapphires warded off depression, jasper helped to prevent fevers, and turquoise held witches at bay. The mother of a newborn child would sometimes don a necklace made of jet and horn to protect herself as well

The manlike form of a mandrake is romanticized in this fifteenth-century drawing, which shows a dog being used to harvest the plant.

as her infant. The woman might also place a piece of iron under the cradle pillow in an effort to ward off evil spirits.

For centuries, the Romanies have been noted for their apparent ability to look into the future—indeed, the Gypsy palm readers and fortunetellers studying their cards and gazing into their crystal balls are the very stereotypes of this ethnic group. In the late nineteenth century, one Gypsy in particular, Urania Boswell, was renowned in England for her gift of prophecy. In 1897, the Romany soothsayer accurately predicted Queen Victoria's death four years hence; she foretold that one day people would fly and would travel underwater in submarines and that they would sit in their parlors listening to voices coming from thousands of miles away. When the *Titanic* was about to embark on its maiden voyage in April of 1912, Boswell allegedly warned one of her clients to cancel his passage. According to the story, the unlucky man ignored the Gypsy's grim advice and thus was among the 1,500 passengers who perished when the vessel went down after striking an iceberg in the North Atlantic.

Gypsies call the power of forecast their second sight. The gift is thought to be fully developed in only a special few, but many Gypsies believe that they possess the ability to varying degrees and can—with proper magical assistance—foresee at least bits and pieces of the future. A pregnant woman may seek advance information on the birth of her child by stringing flowers to a willow twig that has been cut on Saint George's Eve (April 22). Beneath this garland she places an item of her clothing and leaves it there overnight. If a leaf falls on the piece of clothing, the childbirth will go smoothly. Similarly, a girl might attempt to learn whether she will be lucky in love by threading onto her shoelace a stone with a hole in it, then throwing the shoe in a tree. According to Gypsy lore, she can count on being happily married within a year if the shoe catches in the tree. To discover whether her future husband will be young or old, she can mix apple seeds with newly plowed earth and place them at a crossroads on Easter Sunday. If a man is the first one to step on the seeds, her husband will be young; if a woman steps on the seeds first, the girl's mate will be old.

Gypsy women have at least two ways to divine the identities of their husbands to be. The simpler method is to eat an apple—acquired from a widow—on Saint Andrew's Eve (November 29). Half of the apple must be consumed before midnight and the other half after; in her dreams later that night, the woman will see the face of her future spouse. In the more complicated method, the woman stitches into a bag a rabbit's front left paw, three quartz chips, rosemary, rue, some cloth dipped in pigeon's blood, and straw from wheat, oat, barley, and rye. The Gypsy's future husband will be revealed to her in a dream on the first night of the new astrological year if she sleeps on the bag.

It is fashionable in today's sophisticated world of science and all things rational to scoff at much about the belief in low magic. And it is, in fact, quite easy to dismiss offhandedly the inexplicable. Nonetheless, few people in modern society would be prepared to argue that there is no such thing as luck.

Billions upon billions of dollars are wagered each year on the perception of good or bad luck—on the roll of the die, the turn of a card, the spin of the wheel, the outcome of a horse race or some other sporting event. And what gambler does not seek out a way to improve his odds? Twentieth-century culture is replete with its own superstitions and magic designed to attract good fortune or repel ill chance. People carefully throw salt over their left shoulder, knock three times on wood, cross their fingers, step over the cracks on the sidewalk, and assiduously watch themselves when the calendar turns up Friday the thirteenth. They consult astrologers and devour their daily newspaper horoscopes, wear copper wristbands in an effort to ward off rheumatism, hang bronzed baby shoes from their rearview mirrors, jingle with charm bracelets, carry lucky pennies, wear certain clothes at certain times, refuse to shave—or shave their whole heads—rub rabbits' feet, and hang horseshoes over doors.

A woman may adore pearls, but she should not buy them for herself, because that, it is thought, will bring tears. Standing under the mistletoe at Christmas supposedly guarantees a kiss, while eating black-eyed peas on New Year's Day is good medicine for the months ahead. Many a pilot worries about the gremlins that may affect his or her aircraft. And what is a strident "go to Hell" or "God damn you" if not a curse?

Charles Bowness, a longtime researcher into Romany magic, likes to tell the story of a visit from a woman of high intelligence and impressive academic credentials. In the course of a conversation with her, the woman professed herself to be a rational individual and an atheist, and she firmly declared that superstition was all nonsense and the supernatural was simply an outcome of primitive hysteria.

Rising to depart, however, the woman knocked over her handbag, and from it spilled, among other things, a small figurine of a black cat. "Oh," exclaimed the lady, stooping swiftly to retrieve her prized lucky possession, "I must not lose that."

This example is not so dramatic, perhaps, as some Haitian or Hawaiian or Romany amulet, but it is not so different, either.

Amulets to Draw Good Fortune

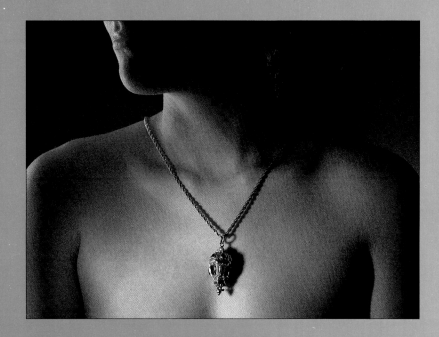

From the dawn of human culture, people have believed in the powers of certain objects to protect against evil and bring good fortune. Amulets, as such items are called, come in myriad forms, but students of the occult classify them in two broad categories—personal and general. As the names suggest, a personal amulet serves its holder exclusively, while a general one protects a wider sphere, such as a household or an entire village.

To some extent, the sorts of objects chosen for amulets have changed along with the evolving world-view of the peoples investing their trust in the charms. The earliest examples tended to be unusual objects found in nature or relics of creatures endowed with desirable traits. These reflected the prevailing sense of many primitive cultures that an invisible force controlled the world and infused everything in nature. As the notion of deities began to take hold, people started fashioning amulets of their own invention— ones that symbolized the powers associated with the divinities that they venerated. Whatever the world-view or the form of the charm, the essence of most amuletic magic—as in many other types of magic—lies in the ancient principle of similarities: People believe that like produces like and that effects will resemble their cause.

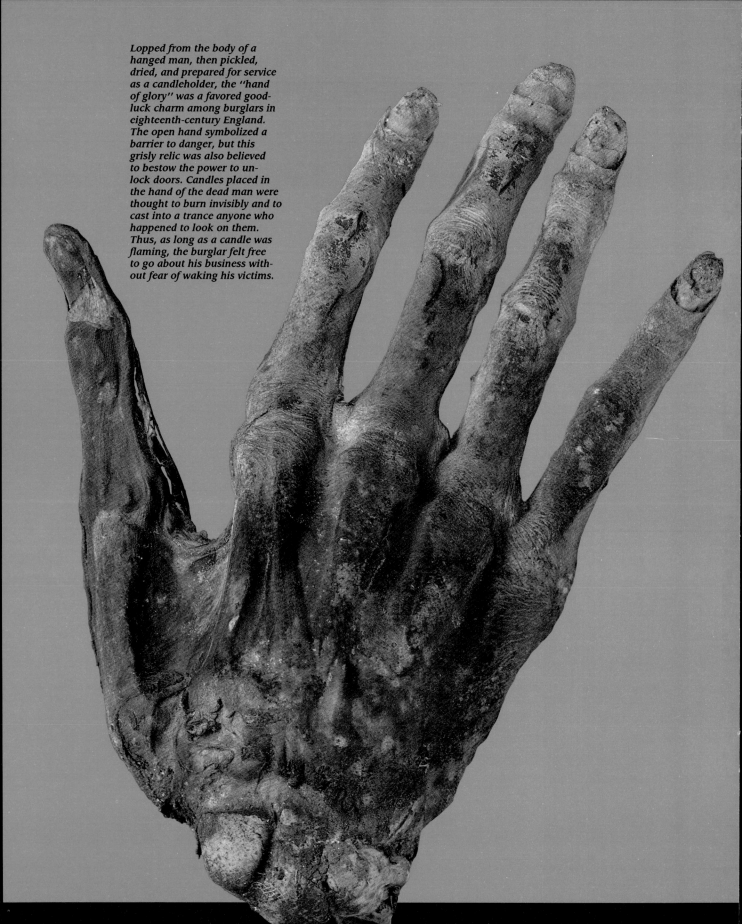

Lopped from the body of a hanged man, then pickled, dried, and prepared for service as a candleholder, the "hand of glory" was a favored good-luck charm among burglars in eighteenth-century England. The open hand symbolized a barrier to danger, but this grisly relic was also believed to bestow the power to unlock doors. Candles placed in the hand of the dead man were thought to burn invisibly and to cast into a trance anyone who happened to look on them. Thus, as long as a candle was flaming, the burglar felt free to go about his business without fear of waking his victims.

This seventeenth-century German bear-tooth rattle with its brass-whistle handle and tinkly bells was an amulet that doubled as a teether. The magical qualities of the rattle were thought to derive from the bear's tooth, which invoked the strength of that powerful animal to ensure good health for the child's teeth. Protective powers were attributed to the teeth of wild animals because of the way the beasts bared their fangs when cornered or threatened. Teeth have also been associated with rites of passage, because baby teeth appear, grow, fall out, and then are replaced by adult teeth.

Enigmatic in form and function, this decorative pitcher made in 1570 by German artist Wenzel Jamnitzer combines a jumble of highly symbolic elements that suggest its use as a personal amulet rather than simply as an object of art. The large, polished snail shells, imported from Formosa, carry connotations of spring and renewal but may also have been used to call upon the healing powers of the sea. Other evocative shapes are cast in the gilded-silver mountings of the shells: A snake-tailed sphinx forms the pitcher's neck, while an eagle depicted in battle with six serpents makes up its base.

A small figure of Bacchus tops this seventeenth-century bezoar amulet from Germany. Sometimes referred to as organ stones, bezoars are hard clumps formed in the intestines of goats and other cud-chewing animals. They have long been prized for their supposed power to counteract food poisoning, accidental or otherwise. At nearly five inches in diameter, this specimen from the stomach of a camel is unusually large —and thus particularly valued.

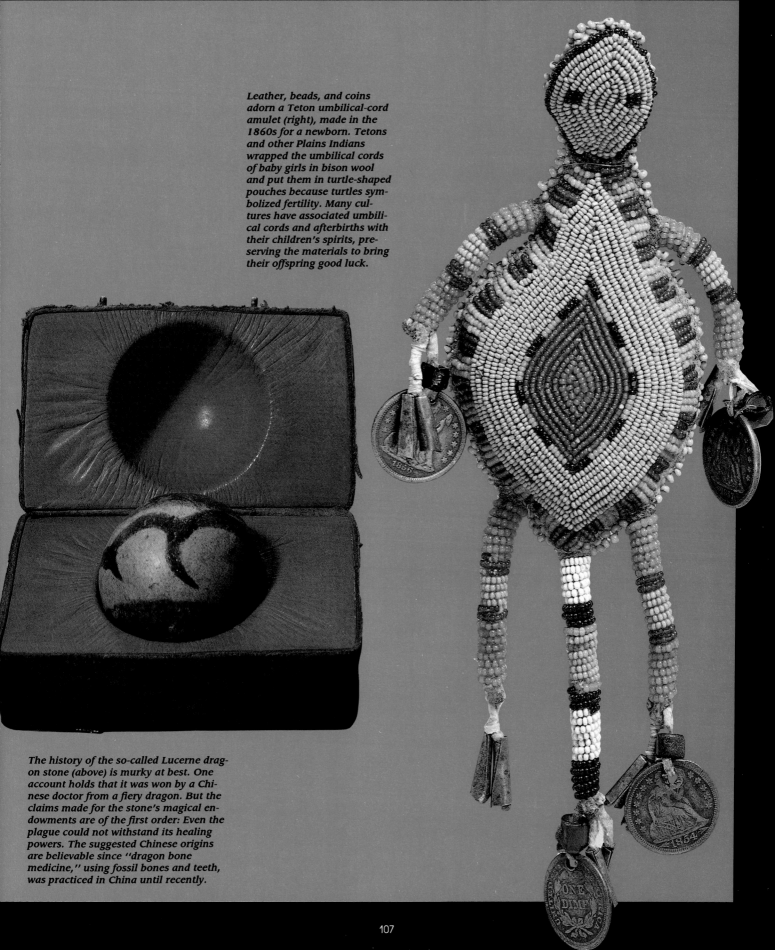

Leather, beads, and coins
adorn a Teton umbilical-cord
amulet (right), made in the
1860s for a newborn. Tetons
and other Plains Indians
wrapped the umbilical cords
of baby girls in bison wool
and put them in turtle-shaped
pouches because turtles symbolized fertility. Many cultures have associated umbilical cords and afterbirths with
their children's spirits, pre-
serving the materials to bring
their offspring good luck.

The history of the so-called Lucerne dragon stone (above) is murky at best. One
account holds that it was won by a Chinese doctor from a fiery dragon. But the
claims made for the stone's magical en-
dowments are of the first order: Even the
plague could not withstand its healing
powers. The suggested Chinese origins
are believable since "dragon bone
medicine," using fossil bones and teeth,
was practiced in China until recently.

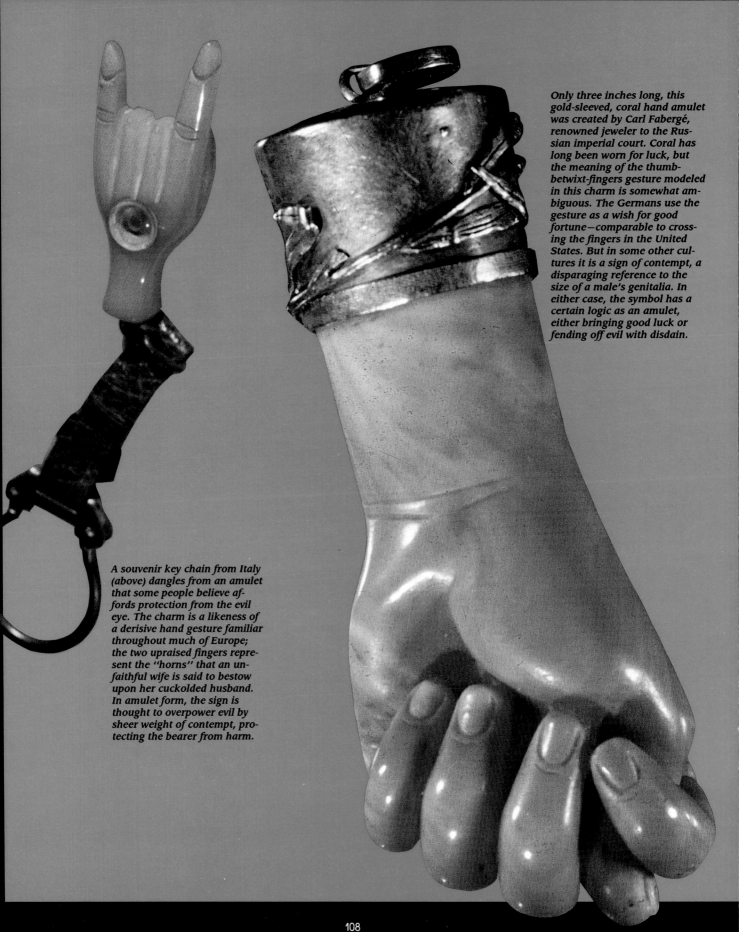

Only three inches long, this gold-sleeved, coral hand amulet was created by Carl Fabergé, renowned jeweler to the Russian imperial court. Coral has long been worn for luck, but the meaning of the thumb-betwixt-fingers gesture modeled in this charm is somewhat ambiguous. The Germans use the gesture as a wish for good fortune—comparable to crossing the fingers in the United States. But in some other cultures it is a sign of contempt, a disparaging reference to the size of a male's genitalia. In either case, the symbol has a certain logic as an amulet, either bringing good luck or fending off evil with disdain.

A souvenir key chain from Italy (above) dangles from an amulet that some people believe affords protection from the evil eye. The charm is a likeness of a derisive hand gesture familiar throughout much of Europe; the two upraised fingers represent the "horns" that an unfaithful wife is said to bestow upon her cuckolded husband. In amulet form, the sign is thought to overpower evil by sheer weight of contempt, protecting the bearer from harm.

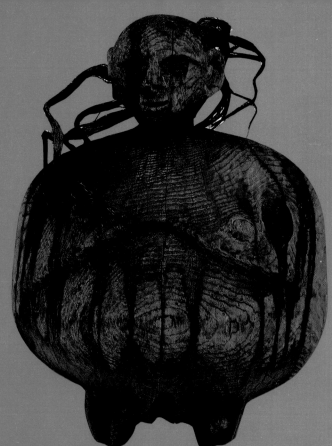

Belly swollen and hands behind her supporting her lower back, this Koniag Indian figurine appears to show a woman in pregnancy or labor, suggesting that it may have been a fertility charm or a birthing amulet. Human hair decorates the carved wooden image, which was discovered in a cache of religious and ceremonial artifacts at a site along the Karluk River on Alaska's Kodiak Island. Archaeologists speculate that the carving may represent one of the many shamanistic spirit helpers that figured in the folk traditions of the Koniags between AD 1500 and 1750.

This amulet, a marten's jaws and menacing teeth encased in silver, was worn in nineteenth-century upper Bavaria to frighten away evil spirits. Hunters also displayed such charms, but they sported them in accordance with the notion that like produces like. With the jaws of large animals or the heads of smaller ones slung from their belts, they believed that they could magically take possession of the strength, ferocity, and cunning of their prey.

Magic in the Modern World

or nine years, even through the bitter length of World War II, the city of Oldham, near Manchester in the northwest of England, had supported a fine repertory theater company. Now, for its ninth anniversary, the troupe had decided to repay the city with a production of William Shakespeare's dark and powerful play *Macbeth*. It was mid-January of 1947, and with two weeks left until opening night, rehearsals were well under way.

British actor Harold Norman was cast as the ambitious, treacherous Macbeth, who murdered his king so as to succeed him. One afternoon, relaxing in a dressing room, Norman began to recite from the play. An older actor, alarmed almost to tears, pleaded with him to stop, reminding him of the "curse of Macbeth," the old theatrical tradition that speaking lines from *Macbeth* anywhere but onstage brings the direst bad luck. But Harold Norman, thirty-four years old and in his prime in those happy postwar days, was not concerned about superstition. He and his wife, a dancer, had a new baby daughter. He was popular with the troupe and with its audience and was pleased and challenged by his current role. Brushing aside his companion's warnings, scoffing at the curse, Norman went on with his recitation.

The production opened on January 27 to good notices. Norman, in the lead, was especially impressive, and if he thought of the curse at all that night, it must have been with a shrug. Three nights later, however, came a bizarre mishap. While director Douglas Emery watched as usual from the wings, Norman and Antony Oakley, the actor playing Macduff, fought out their climactic battle to the death with sword and dagger. Although the two had planned and rehearsed their bloody duel meticulously, something went askew, and both men lacked their accustomed grace. At last Oakley made his killing lunge, and Norman crashed to the floor. But instead of acting Macbeth's death onstage, Norman extemporized a halting crawl to the wings. There he whispered up to the director, "I've been stabbed, and I can't take my curtain call."

In the staged fight, Oakley's blunted weapon had somehow broken through Norman's costume and pierced his abdomen. An ambulance was summoned, even as the audience clamored for the star to reappear. Director

Emery slipped through the curtain, quieted the house, and explained what had happened. Harold Norman could not take his bow because he was wounded—although, it appeared, not gravely.

In fact, the wound called for surgery; the dagger had perforated Norman's bowel. The local newspaper played down the accident, unwilling to sensationalize it with references to the legendary curse of Macbeth. No one mentioned the incident of two weeks earlier, when Norman had defied the curse. The show did go on, with a substitute actor playing the part of Macbeth. The patient seemed to be recovering well, and everyone assumed he would soon return to the company. But then his progress slackened, and peritonitis—a general infection of the abdomen—took hold. One month after he had been stabbed onstage, Harold Norman died.

An inquest determined that the weapon involved was blunted in the usual way and that Antony Oakley bore no grudge against the deceased. Oakley was ex-onerated and Norman's death was ruled an accident. Unfortunately, however, the sad events connected with the Oldham production of *Macbeth* were not yet over. Soon afterward, Harold Norman's infant daughter died of suffocation in the actors' lodgings, and his widow, overcome by her two terrible losses, suffered a nervous breakdown and gave up performing.

Not for a quarter century did the story of Harold Norman's offstage recitation come out. So wary of this play are some actors, so seriously do they take the so-called curse of Macbeth, that few members of the Oldham theater company would discuss even the onstage accident, let alone the scene in the dressing room.

Actors are a superstitious lot—a fact most of them will readily acknowledge. As almost everyone knows, theater folk even consider it bad luck to wish good luck to anyone about to perform. They much prefer to hear, "Break a leg!" or perhaps, "Fall down backwards!" But irrational beliefs are certainly not confined to one side of the foot-

One of many actors allegedly hexed by a curse associated with
Shakespeare's Macbeth, Sir Herbert Beerbohm Tree—here with Constance Collier in
a 1916 film adaptation—lost his Hollywood contract after starring in the
title role. Believers in the curse note that all prints of the movie have somehow disappeared.

lights. Every audience, too, has its superstitious members—believers in lucky numbers, lucky days, or simply in luck itself. And should one playgoer sneeze, another is sure to exclaim, "Bless you!" This common custom, which to most people does not seem like a superstition, in fact comes from the old belief that with the violent breath, the soul of the person was expelled. A quick blessing was needed to prevent the devil from taking possession of the temporarily vacant body.

Superstition, based on the notion that supernatural forces of a non-religious character can intervene in real life, is a form of belief in magic. Around the world, the number of people who are loyal to ancient magical ideas is striking. Magic is alive, and the persistence of superstition is just one of the ways—albeit, probably the most common and widespread way—in which it continues to thrive at the heart of present-day culture.

Magic has many manifestations in the landscape of modern life. One is the recent resurgence of witchcraft—called Wicca by its devotees—with its reliance on rituals, charms, and spells to work for psychic and physical changes. Less systematic but far more pervasive is the magic

Children tie rags called clooties to trees near a spring in Scotland. The act is akin to tossing coins in a well and may have originated in earlier customs for appeasing the spirits in pools. The word clooties is derived from a Scottish name for the devil.

glimpsed in advertisements. "Wear this football player's brand of underwear"—so goes the implied promise—"and you will share in his strength and power." In a sense, the popular pastime of betting on lotteries involves a kind of belief in magic. The millions-to-one odds make winning a lotto jackpot next to impossible, yet many fans are secretly convinced that a magical scheme or force—the finger of fate, no less—has ordained that they will overcome the odds; they simply have to keep buying tickets so as not to deny fate its opportunity to touch them. In many cases they try to work their own magic spells by selecting combinations of numbers that they believe to be lucky.

The words *magic* and *superstition* are not neutral terms; people have long used them as weapons for bashing one another's beliefs, and a wide variety of phenomena are labeled magical by their critics. In some quarters, belief in magic is held to be religion or science "gone wrong." Nonbelievers apply the term *superstition* to many religious faiths. Unorthodoxy is not even required; unfamiliarity has long been sufficient to call forth the epithet. The eighteenth-century French philosopher Voltaire observed: "A Frenchman traveling in Italy finds almost everything superstitious and is hardly wrong. The archbishop of Canterbury claims that the archbishop of Paris is superstitious; the Presbyterians levy the same reproach against his Grace of Canterbury, and are in their turn called superstitious by the Quakers, who are the most superstitious of men in the eyes of other Christians." Much depends, of course, on who is doing the labeling. To an atheist, any belief at all in any higher power is magical thinking and superstition.

Similarly, much that is unorthodox in medicine is branded as fringe science, magical and superstitious pseudoscience. For example, most scientists regard megavitamins, those nutrients packaged in very large doses—and much else that is found in health-food stores—as magical nonsense. Alternative therapies, such as homeopathy, acupuncture, and chiropractic, are often decried by their critics as quackery or as magic, in the pejorative sense.

On the other hand, some traditional practices that were formerly dismissed as mere superstition—as foolish, groundless beliefs—have turned out to have provable value. A simple example is the Jewish mother's age-old conviction that eating chicken soup provides relief from the common cold. The concoction really does help some of the sufferer's symptoms, and when the fragrant steam from the hot broth is inhaled through the nose, it relieves nasal congestion. Moreover, social scientists concede that certain communal magical practices can have latent functions, or unanticipated benefits, which explain why people cling to them so tenaciously. The Hopi rain dance, for instance, can provide the very real benefits of group solidarity and cohesion during a time of crisis, even if it does not produce any immediate relief from drought.

In spite of scientists' dogged efforts at debunking them, many occult, or "hidden," subjects, including magic,

Colorful hex signs ornament a barn in the heart of the Pennsylvania Dutch country. Such emblems, ubiquitous in the region, are nowadays prized mainly for their decorative value, but at one time they were believed to protect families and livestock from witchcraft. Some people still regard the signs as charms. Common designs include stars (inset, top), which signify fertility, abundance, and success in life, and rosettes (inset, bottom), which are reputed to attract prosperity, luck, and physical well-being.

have an apparently increasing appeal in this century. There is much interest among educated urbanites, for example, in the supposedly magical practices of ethnic sorcerers such as the Yaqui Indian Don Juan (who was alleged to be a real-life magician in the popular books of author Carlos Castaneda but who was later debunked as a total fabrication by the investigative work of Richard de Mille). To cope with the myriad stresses of life, many modern Western people have set out deliberately to rediscover and embrace the most primitive roots of magic. Interest has mushroomed in the healing powers of shamanism *(pages 66-75)*, the ancient mystical practices of tribal peoples. New Age bookshelves groan under the weight of the latest volumes on old, nonrational systems of divination, such as Tarot-card reading and numerology. And some New Age practitioners consult the movements of a pendulum to choose among the various healing remedies.

These age-old magical practices have drawn a growing minority of new adherents, many of whom are willing to study long and hard to acquire the traditional tools of mag-

Unusual cone-roofed houses called trulli, found on southern Italy's Adriatic coast, are painted with special symbols in order to fend off the evil eye.

ic, both high and low. But one powerful manifestation of magic, superstition—acquired without study, almost without awareness—makes its way silently and unbidden into almost every consciousness, thus affecting the lives of even those who would deny harboring any superstitious beliefs.

The curse of Macbeth, like other magical and superstitious beliefs, arose not out of thin air but from real events. Misfortune has all too often struck productions of *Macbeth*, beginning with its very first performance, in 1606. The boy who was to play Lady Macbeth (in accord with the custom of the time, which excluded women from the acting profession) fell ill, and the playwright himself had to step into the role for the play's premiere.

The play had been commissioned by King James I of England, to entertain his royal Danish in-laws during a state visit. To mark the occasion, Shakespeare chose to write not another of his popular, sunny comedies but a doom-laden drama of witchcraft and treason in James's native Scotland.

King James was a squeamish, nervous man, fearful of witchcraft and painfully aware that his political enemies might decide to kill him, as they had killed three of his relatives. He disliked the play so much that he banned it for the next five years.

When performances started up again, the play quickly developed its ominous reputation. Whenever it was presented, according to the growing legend, there were strange mishaps: Scenery fell, actors misstepped, people in the company took sick, and bad luck seemed to be everywhere. *Macbeth*, actors began to declare, was a cursed play, and the belief gathered strength over the centuries. In 1937, Sir Laurence Olivier narrowly escaped with his life when a twenty-five-pound stage weight fell from overhead, demolishing a chair that he had vacated just seconds before.

Of course, not all of the play's mishaps are quite so sinister. One production, done outdoors before a castle on a wind-swept promontory in Bermuda in 1953, suffered a piece of bad luck so absurd that its audience dissolved in helpless laughter. The staging of Lady Macbeth's suicide called for a stagehand to toss a costumed dummy over the cliff—to a place from which it would later be retrieved for the next performance. During one ill-starred performance, a capricious wind seized the falling body and tossed it right back up onto solid ground. In this particular case, no one was injured, but artistically, the mood of the play was shattered beyond repair.

Still, the years have freighted *Macbeth* with a lore and superstition that make it unique among Shakespeare's plays. Many researchers document the curse of Macbeth, and even today some actors can reel off a catalog of misadventures and troubled performances to support their belief in the curse.

Tradition blames the drama's supposed malignancy on the spell chanted by the witches in act 4, scene 1, of the play. The incantation's horrific images and chilling words— "Scale of dragon, tooth of wolf, Witch's mummy, maw and gulf"—were not Shakespeare's own, according to the lore. Allegedly the playwright lifted them from rituals then in common use by real and thriving practitioners of witchcraft in the English countryside.

From the play's earliest days, it has always been considered bad luck to speak or even refer to the weird sisters' curse anywhere but onstage during a performance. Eventually, this prohibition grew to embrace the entire play, including even its name. Many actors avoid saying the title, *Macbeth,* calling it instead The Unmentionable, or The Scottish Play, or simply That Play.

Although the fear of reciting from That Play is alleged to originate in real events, many superstitious beliefs are so old that the reasons behind them are all but forgotten. But the word *superstition* itself contains a clue to the origins of some customs that bear the name. It comes from the Latin words *super,* meaning "above," and *stare,* meaning "to stand"; originally, the *superstite* was the warrior left standing above the bodies of his dead enemies. In the realm of belief and behavior, then, a superstition is a custom that lives on after the demise of the belief system, or religion, in which it belonged.

In human history, the first belief systems were based on magic and on deities now superseded by others. It is these early beliefs that can still be seen at the root of many superstitions today. Developed to account for the randomness and seeming cruelty of events, such beliefs have three key premises: that unseen powers are at work in the happenings of the visible world; that these powers can and do manipulate human lives; and that humans in turn can manipulate the invisible powers, by propitiating, flattering, or fooling them. What originally developed as religious magic to speak to these spirits lingers today in the form of some of the world's most widespread superstitions.

One nearly universal practice is knocking on wood. All sorts of people knock on wood the moment they say they are pleased with something. In answer to a question, a patient will say, "Doc, I feel great," or a shopkeeper will say, "Business is booming"—then both will immediately knock

Recipes for Love Potions

In days past, recipes for philters—magic love potions—were known for their esoteric or unappealing ingredients. A strapping lad or beauteous maid had to be either unaware of the contents or very thirsty to sip a potion with brain of blackbird or human blood.

A present-day mixer of philters, a self-described witch named Gundella who lives in Michigan, takes a more practical approach than her forebears in sorcery. Her teas, sweets, and heartier tidbits, a few of which are described below, contrive to be attractive and tasty. The ingredients can be found in a supermarket, and most of the recipes are easy to prepare. One calls not for a cauldron but for a microwave oven. Despite their convenience, Gundella asserts, her concoctions have real magical power because they use herbs and spices long known for their effects in matters of love.

The Rose Hips Tea is meant to inspire tender feelings; the Love Apple Cocktail is meant to arouse desire. To encourage commitment or recapture a straying partner, Gundella suggests her Rocky Road Romancer; for playful passion, the savory Hanky Panky.

Rose Hips Tea

Prepare 4 cups of rose hips tea following the directions on the package, but add 1/2 teaspoon of catnip and 1/8 teaspoon of crushed rosemary. Let the tea steep for 8 to 10 minutes, then strain it and serve unsweetened or with honey. Roses, long associated with love and beauty, and rosemary, which has been related to fidelity, are the key ingredients here.

Love Apple Cocktail

Stir together in a saucepan 2 cups of tomato juice, 1 bay leaf, 1 teaspoon of basil, and a dash each of dill and Worcestershire sauce. Simmer the mixture for three minutes, then chill it in a refrigerator. Strain the beverage before serving. Dill is purportedly powerful enough to bring on proposals of marriage, so you may wish to substitute celery salt unless your intentions are serious.

Rocky Road Romancer

Combine 12 ounces of semisweet chocolate chips, 12 ounces of butterscotch chips, and 1 cup of peanut butter in a bowl. Microwave the ingredients for four minutes or melt them in a double boiler. Fold in 10 1/2 ounces of miniature marshmallows and 1 1/2 cups of salted peanuts. Spread this mixture in a buttered 9-by-13-inch pan and refrigerate until set. Adding a teaspoon of cinnamon to the fudge may inspire a marriage proposal.

Hanky Panky

Combine 1/2 pound of ground beef, 1/2 pound of pork sausage, 1/2 pound of shredded cheddar cheese, 1/2 teaspoon of oregano, and 1/2 teaspoon of garlic powder in a bowl, then spread this pâté on small thin slices of rye or pumpernickel bread. Cook the open-faced sandwiches under a broiler until the meat is well browned. The oregano and garlic charge the pâté with passion.

on wood, or, in Great Britain, touch wood and whistle. Boasting invites disaster, so the belief goes, and one should call on wood for protection. Some people may say that the gesture invokes the powers of the true cross, the most powerful of Christian relics. But the practice is older than that, and originally it was done to summon the protective powers of tree gods.

Tossing spilled salt over the left shoulder to avert bad luck is another ancient custom, perhaps nearly as old—and nearly as widespread—as salt in the human diet. As the earliest preservative, a primary seasoning, and a vital nutrient, salt was recognized ages ago as one of the essential ingredients of life. Common sense would agree that to spill salt was to lose a precious commodity and should arouse anxiety. But why, once spilled, should salt be thrown over the left shoulder? Because it is there that evil spirits perch—or so the ancients believed—awaiting their chance for mischief, and the salt thrown in their eyes would put them out of commission for those few perilous moments. Those same evil spirits, it was thought, sought every opportunity to zip into the body through any of its openings—and not only after a sneeze—to take it over. The first earrings were probably worn to bar the way to these spirits, and so was the first lipstick.

Horseshoes have been regarded as good-luck charms perhaps since the first ones were made thousands of years ago. After all, they were forged of sacred iron in sacred fire, in the shape of the sacred crescent moon. A rabbit's foot is another good-luck charm in many parts of the world. Its alleged powers are based on a kind of contagious magic, bringing the creature's qualities to the carrier of the charm. Of course, the rabbit's legendary powers of procreation promise prosperity to the owner. But rabbits were also said to be born with their eyes open and thus able to recognize the devil from their first moments.

Black cats, though worshiped in ancient Egypt, came to be bad omens in the Middle Ages through their alleged double lives as the familiars, or magical partners, of witches. Curiously, however, in Great Britain a pure black cat is a very auspicious sign. During World War II, Britain's prime minister Winston Churchill made a point of stroking black cats at every opportunity, and some people believe this brought him the good luck he needed to pull his country through that conflict.

On the matter of breaking a mirror, superstitious opinion is not divided. Only bad luck can follow, doubtless because a mirror contains its owner's image, and whatever happens to the likeness is believed to portend the same for the original. In fact, if a mirror—or, worse yet, a person's portrait—should fall from its place on a wall, it is widely seen as an omen of death.

With similar lack of ambivalence, many people will go out of their way to avoid walking under a ladder, to escape a pervasive bad luck that extends well beyond possible damage from falling paint or tools. Perhaps the dread attached to ladders goes back to an early kind of gallows, a horizontal pole with a noose attached, which required the victim to climb a ladder to attend his own hanging.

Even a color can become taboo. Theater people avoid wearing green onstage, perhaps for the sound technical reason that green is difficult to light in a flattering way. But some say it is because green is the color of fairies, sprites, and leprechauns, and these beings will surely cause mischief to anybody else who wears their hue.

And it is not only theater folk who believe so. One woman in Surrey, England, gave up her job with a caterer after eight years rather than wear the company's new green uniform. The firm had been pleased with her work and promised to hire her back if ever they changed the color of their uniform. Superstitious fear of green has even invaded the scientific precincts of the National Aeronautics and Space Administration. The unlucky color was carefully excluded by the astronauts of the *Apollo 13* moon mission, which was launched on April 11, 1970. Despite this precaution, the mission was cut short anyway, when an on-board oxygen tank exploded two days later—on the thirteenth. Some onlookers said an accident

Bracketed by two upright stones that may have been used for astronomical sightings, the Men-an-Tol, a holed megalith in Cornwall, has long been prized for its alleged healing powers. As late as the 1800s, people crawled through the opening in a symbolic act of rebirth to cure lumbago, sciatica, and cricks in the back. Children with rickets, it was said, were healed when passed nine times through the hole.

was virtually guaranteed because of the mission's unlucky number—thirteen.

Fear of the number thirteen is a near-universal superstition, traced by many to the Last Supper. At that meal, the treacherous Judas, having already agreed to turn Jesus over to the Roman soldiers who would later crucify him, was the thirteenth guest. Scandinavian myth tells of a feast of the gods at which the thirteenth guest, the mischievous Loki, caused the death of the beloved Balder, god of light and joy. In any event, millions of people today count their dinner guests carefully to avoid having a party of one more than twelve. London's elegant Savoy Hotel keeps a special over-size figure of a black cat, complete with a bib, ready to occupy a fourteenth chair for any dinner party anxious to avoid the number thirteen. The number is thought so unlucky that hotels avoid having a thirteenth floor. Their floor numbers skip from twelve to fourteen.

Friday the thirteenth is doubly unlucky, combining the baleful number with Friday, the day on which Christ died. Throughout the Middle Ages, Friday was also the hangman's day, the regular day for executions of criminals. Few businessmen today will plan to start a new enterprise on any Friday, and many expect the worst in the stock market every Friday the thirteenth.

While all of these observances are acknowledged as superstitions, certain other practices, too, are based on out-dated beliefs and qualify as superstitions, although people performing them may not know it. The laying of a corner-stone, for instance, is a happy scene in civic and business life. A real-estate developer, a handful of bankers, and several insurance executives pose proudly with the mayor for pictures while a time capsule filled with mementos of the day is mortared into the cornerstone of a new office tower. But how many of the participants understand that the tradition of the cornerstone goes back to ancient and grisly rites? In some cultures of the past, including ancient Rome, the collapse of a new building was not blamed on faulty engineering; instead, it was attributed to the wrath of the spirits who dwelled in the earth and were disturbed by the structure. To buy off these spirits, the builders sacrificed people—in some cases, children—and buried them at the corners of new constructions. Eventually animals took the place of human sacrifices, and now, in a rite still surrounded with great ceremony, newspaper clippings and other homely oddments of everyday life are most likely to be the items builders enclose at the corner of a new building.

Once the cornerstone is laid, many builders fear the worst if a news article is published about a building before its completion. This reaction is an updated version of the ancient belief that boasting attracts punishment; however, it carries no escape clause—no chance to knock on wood for safety. After the collapse of a bridge under construction in Australia in the early 1970s, a prominent builder told a reporter, apparently in all seriousness: "I don't think the King's Bridge at Melbourne would have collapsed if the engineer hadn't written a series of articles about the design. The ink was hardly dry before the bridge fell in the drink."

Those omnipresent, malicious spirits that people

dodge, court, and appease through superstitious behavior apparently reserve perfection for themselves. If they discover perfection in the human realm, so the belief goes, they inflict a jealous and destructive revenge, and many customs are practiced to head off just these attacks. Potters have been known to create a deliberate flaw—a thumbprint, perhaps—on a perfectly thrown pot before setting it in the kiln, as a means of protecting it from the spirits' jealous destructiveness during the firing. And actors, in their bag of superstitions, naturally have a method for dealing with the perils of perfection. To avoid a perfect rehearsal, which would invite disaster during the performance, they leave every rehearsal incomplete, never speaking the last line of the show except to finish an actual performance. There is, unfortunately, no such countermagic for the rather helpless feeling that many automobile owners share, that the shine on a newly washed car attracts the rain that spoils it.

Luckily, these same jealous and vindictive spirits seem to be susceptible to the power of suggestion; they can be conned into imitating the behavior of humans. Thus a sober, responsible, and otherwise rational stockbroker in Washington, D.C., is known to hold up his trousers with both a belt and suspenders on days when he feels prices on the New York Stock Exchange are in danger of a downward slide and could benefit from some extra support.

Superstitions involving automobiles and stock markets are among a handful that have clearly modern origins. Another is the conviction that lighting three cigarettes on the same match will bring catastrophe to one of the smokers. Three, of course, has had magical meanings for millennia; the ancient Greeks performed many rituals three times, and good things, as well as bad news, are often said to come in threes. The bad luck of three on a match, however, dates back only to the Boer War, fought at the beginning of the twentieth century. The British soldiers serving in South Africa faced formidable sharpshooters in their Afrikaner enemies. For Tommies on guard at night, keeping a match lit long enough to light three cigarettes could have given a sniper the time he needed to aim and fire at the third smoker.

Although no one knows exactly where it originated, perhaps the oldest and most widespread of superstitions is belief in the so-called evil eye. Millions of people all over the world are convinced that certain persons can do evil to others merely by a malevolent glance. This conviction girdles the globe—from the Near East, where it is thought to have started in pre-Christian times, through Europe and the Americas and across Asia. And even though it is strongest in rural communities, the belief is remarkably consistent wherever it occurs.

The feared power is thought to emanate from someone's eye and to strike persons, animals, or objects with sudden destruction or injury. The victim may succumb, it is said, to an accident or acute illness—or perhaps a lingering, wasting disease. Animals will sicken and die, abort their unborn young, or stop giving milk or laying eggs. In one Greek village, the tale was told of a fine old olive press that once split in half without warning, only moments after a passing stranger glanced at it covetously.

The evil eye is expected to attack anything valuable enough to be admired and envied. Envy and greed have been seen as evil partners for millennia. In the Bible, a verse in Proverbs notes, "He that hath an evil eye hasteneth after riches." Indeed, the last of the Ten Commandments is an injunction against envy: "Thou shalt not covet . . . anything that is thy neighbor's." To avoid attracting an envious evil

Four dogs stabbed in the heart, draped with grass collars, and mounted on poles form a grisly barrier on the outskirts of a Koryak Indian village in Siberia around the turn of the century. The sacrifice of dogs —which some say may still be practiced in remote parts of Siberia— was intended to frighten away spirits that might otherwise do harm.

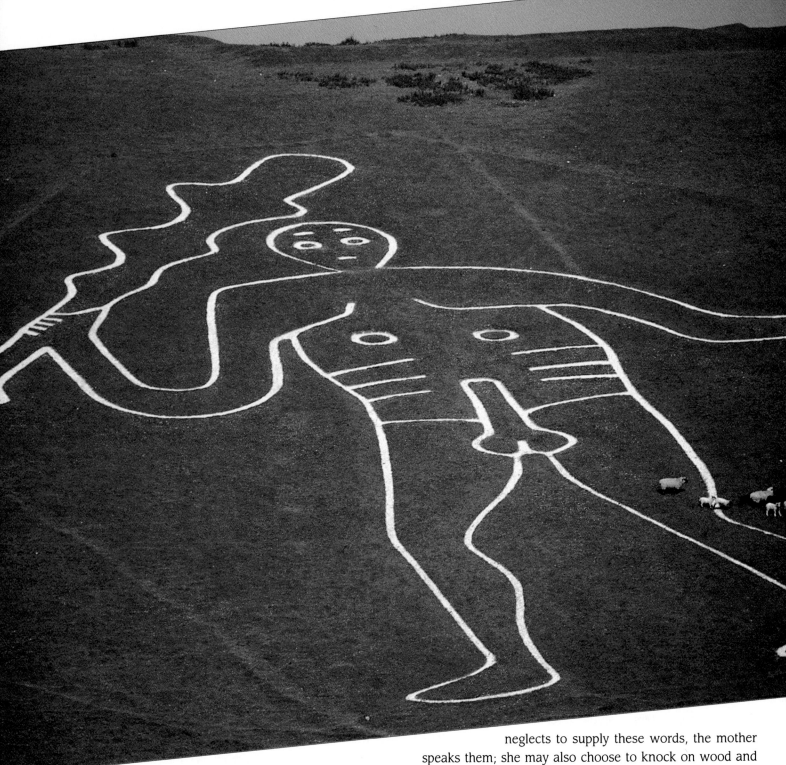

eye, then, one widespread precaution is to take care not to boast. To the question, "How are you?" many a healthy and prosperous Italian will cautiously reply, "Luckily, not bad."

Children, because of their beauty and innocence, are considered prime targets for the evil eye and must be protected. In various cultures, people expressing admiration or praise for a baby must swiftly murmur a magical protection—something like, "An evil eye should not befall him," or simply, "God bless him." If the person admiring the child

neglects to supply these words, the mother speaks them; she may also choose to knock on wood and spit three times.

Americans, rich in a mix of traditional superstitions brought to the New World by immigrants, are not immune to belief in the evil eye—even though the country's numerous psychiatrists offer alternative, psychological explanations to those who blame their troubles on the effects of a baleful glare. The clash between these competing views attracted attention as early as the 1930s in a case involving a Boston housewife to whom researchers gave the pseudonym Angelina Perella.

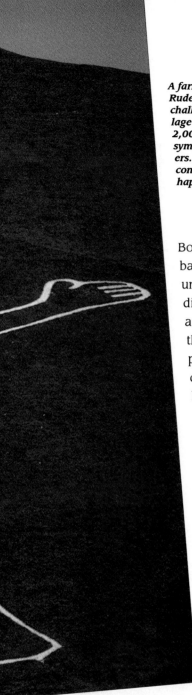

Both Mrs. Perella and her husband had been born in Italy, but unlike her spouse, she had had a difficult time learning English and had remained attached to the old values and beliefs still prevalent in parts of the mother country. She was, in her husband's view, "practical rather than imaginative" yet at the same time "unusually superstitious." When she became pregnant with their ninth child, she began to express whims that Mr. Perella attempted to indulge, even to the extent of purchasing and slaughtering a live pig so she could drink its blood. The delivery of the couple's baby went well enough, with mother and child both doing fine. But less than a week after giving birth, Mrs. Perella started behaving strangely. She laid her troubles to a hospital visit from a neighbor, Mrs. J, as the psychiatric records describing Mrs. Perella's case refer to this woman. Indeed, that very evening, Mrs. Perella told her husband that she had fallen under the spell of the evil eye and that it was Mrs. J who had bewitched her. She claimed that Mrs. J was jealous of the attention and gifts that had been showered on her and her new baby.

The records do not reveal Mr. Perella's reaction to his wife's statement, but it may not have struck him as entirely odd, since belief in the evil eye remains a common feature of Italian folklore. However, Mrs. Perella began complaining of being intermittently hot and cold and of feeling poorly. Soon her breast milk dried up. When she returned home, she found four of her children ill and believed that they all might have died had she stayed any longer at the hospital. She attributed the poor state of health within her household to Mrs. J, whom she was soon blaming for every misfortune, real or imagined.

Just as she might have done in the old country, Mrs. Perella tried to counteract the spell. She visited a fortuneteller who gave her what seemed to be useful advice, and for a while her condition improved. But then she developed a mysterious and painful swelling in the arms. She became all the more convinced that she was being victimized by Mrs. J. When the fortuneteller asked her whether Mrs. J had removed any items from her home, Mrs. Perella remembered that she had lent two dresses belonging to one of her daughters to her neighbor and had never gotten them back. Since the little girl had been sick of late, Mrs. Perella concluded that this was yet another indication of the malevolence of Mrs. J, who was using her daughter's clothing to cast a spell on the child.

After her initial success with her client, the fortuneteller grew bolder. She suggested to Mrs. Perella that something blue in her house was contributing to her misfortune. Mrs. Perella conducted a thorough search but could come up only with an American flag, which she washed according to the fortuneteller's instructions.

Again she appeared to improve. But the next time the fortuneteller took things too far: The woman told Mrs. Perella that she would find a tin can filled with money and that they would divide the bounty between them. The following day Mrs. Perella rose at five o'clock in the morning and proceeded to turn her house upside down in a futile search for the money. The desperate woman even went so far as to open up cans of food in the hope that the cash might be concealed with the contents.

When she failed to find the trove, Mrs. Perella panicked; she was convinced that others knew about the money and were going to kidnap her children and hold them for ransom. She locked doors and windows and grew increasingly restless, eating and sleeping little. She spoke of cars circling the house at night with their lights turned off so that she could not see who was driving them and of strangers sneaking in to ransack her home. These very people, she said, had somehow managed to build a fire under her bed, and the heat was keeping her awake. As her condition worsened, her husband had no option but to admit her to a psychiatric hospital.

There, Mrs. Perella's poor English made communication with the staff difficult, although she was able to convey to them that she was hearing inner voices—"head no feel a good, talk a talk a talk." She was diagnosed as a paranoid schizophrenic.

Because Mrs. Perella's condition improved somewhat during a week of treatment, her husband withdrew her from the hospital so that she could be with her family. But five days after her discharge, her schizophrenia—or her belief in the magical power of the evil eye—caught up with her. She answered the doorbell to greet someone who wanted to know the time. The kitchen clock was not working, so Mrs. Perella went upstairs to determine the hour. As nearly as could be gathered afterward, she became confused and, perhaps responding to the commands of hallucinatory voices, took off her clothes and drenched herself with rubbing alcohol, then set herself afire. Grabbing two of her younger children, she held them under her arms and descended the stairs in flames.

The youngsters survived, but Mrs. Perella died of her burns ten days later. Her husband and her psychiatrist believed that mental illness had compelled her bizarre act of self-immolation. Some of her neighbors, however, probably agreed with the interpretation that Mrs. Perella herself had fixed upon, that she was the victim of a cursed glance. Even accepting the psychiatric diagnosis without quibble, it seems entirely possible that Mrs. Perella's fear of the evil eye may have unleashed forces that her troubled psyche was not strong enough to withstand. "The strength of such beliefs is that people can live and die by them," Alan Dundes, a teacher of folklore at the University of California, Berkeley, observed in another, similar context. "People are scared to death of violating their belief structure."

Although some people are believed to cast the evil eye deliberately, others supposedly radiate misfortune without even knowing it. When a mishap or illness does occur, often the first order of business is to decide who is responsible for it—who has cast the evil eye. In Italy and elsewhere, there are people who claim the power to ferret out the evil eye, to point to the source of the problem so that the community can destroy it. Naturally, such a "curer" wields considerable social and political power, and if there is ever an eye truly to be feared, it is that of an unfriendly curer. In the end, the combination of belief in the evil eye as well as a tendency to gossip can wrap a village in a web of surveillance and mutual suspicion. As one rural Italian woman put it, "There is an expression here. Be friends with everyone, but trust no one."

In the face of so much magically caused trouble, innumerable magical defenses have grown up. Mothers in Eastern Europe may attach red ribbons to a baby's clothing, carriage, or crib. An Italian farming family's prize ox may be protected with a red ribbon, this one tied to the fur between its eyes. Strings of garlic draped over doorways and borders of red or blue paint around window frames are thought to protect houses and barns in rural parts of Italy. Many Mediterranean shopkeepers place a bit of iron—a key or a horseshoe—near the door, where they can touch it to ward off the evil of envious glances. People may wear charms of silver, gold, or amber, in the shape of an eye, an open hand, a fish, or—prized for its alleged power to pierce the evil-eye curse and render it harmless—an animal's horn.

Boat owners on Malta paint eyes on the prows of their vessels, and the island's automobiles bear painted eyes on their bumpers or trunk lids. One Greek bus driver was heard to proclaim loudly that he did not believe in the evil eye himself, even though some people said his father had had the power. This driver had painted his bus blue and white, however. While these are the colors of the national flag,

In the quiet Spanish village of Castrillo de Murcia, a
costumed demon leaps over a bed filled with babies. The unique ritual is
believed to guard the young from unkind spirits and—
for some forgotten magical reason—protect them from hernias as well.

In a practice common to Arab lands, the shutters and trim of this Moroccan window are painted sky blue to trick malevolent spirits. Custom holds that demons can function only in darkness and will avoid a dwelling if deceived into thinking it is day.

they are also the colors Greeks use to repel the evil eye. Perhaps the man subscribed to another Mediterranean folk saying: "It is not true. But I believe it."

The power of the evil eye is not very different from the power of a voodoo curse. Both can do real harm, but both depend for their power on the unquestioning belief of their victims. According to Robert T. Smith, a writer who has reported on the occult movement, a young woman who claimed she was under a voodoo curse and who complained of chest pains was admitted to a Baltimore hospital in 1967. Smith's account relates that Martha Fisher (not her real name) told a doctor she was one of three girls born

nearly twenty-three years earlier in the Okefenokee Swamp on a Friday the thirteenth. The voodoo midwife who attended all three deliveries allegedly informed the three mothers that their babies were cursed. "The first will die," the woman predicted, "before her sixteenth birthday. The second will not live to be twenty-one and the third will not see twenty-three."

The story says that the first girl had indeed died in a car accident the day before her sixteenth birthday. And supposedly the second, out to celebrate the failure of the curse against her on her twenty-first birthday, was killed by a stray bullet as she entered a bar. Now Martha Fisher, after puzzling doctors at the hospital with unexplained dizzy spells, shortness of breath, cold sweats, and anxiety, died the day before her twenty-third birthday. "An autopsy showed pulmonary hypertension," Smith pointed out in his book *Cult & Occult,* "which is another way of saying she died of fright."

Just as belief in such a curse can kill, belief in a magical protection has been known to save a life. Had Martha Fisher's doctors been able to convince her that they had cast a counterspell, she might have outlived the malevolent influence she felt herself under.

Many present-day magical or superstitious practices are in the nature of a spell. English-speaking children learn to chant, "Rain, rain, go away, come again another day." And mothers for ages have planted a magical kiss on a child's bumped knee, with the magical words, "Kiss it and make it better." For many people, however, luck is attached not to words but to material objects—lucky charms variously known as talismans, amulets, and mascots. Although most cultures have standard lucky charms—be they red ribbons or rabbits' feet—many people adopt and cling to private talismans and amulets of their own. Still others may take on a more or less complicated routine to be performed when luck is needed. All of these superstitious practices are easy to find among athletes.

To avoid washing away his good luck, former light-heavyweight champion Marvin Johnson would carefully

*Guarding against the evil eye, handprints dot a graffiti-strewn wall
in Tangier, Morocco. The power of the outstretched hand to deflect the vengeful
force of the evil eye is recognized all over northern Africa, as well
as in the Mideast, India, and southern Europe.*

avoid bathing for twenty-four hours before every fight. The Philadelphia Flyers hockey team in the mid-1970s adopted the singer Kate Smith as their lucky mascot, playing her recording of "God Bless America" before their home games: They won an impressive fifty-four out of sixty-five of them. Tennis star Martina Navratilova has made it a point to always wear a certain pair of diamond earrings during tournament play; furthermore, she always calls tails at the opening coin toss that decides who serves first, and for the final day, she always wears a tennis dress of turquoise. When Chris Evert lost a match for which she had donned her lucky yellow tennis dress, her then-beau Jimmy Connors advised her, "Burn the dress."

Baseball's long history has nurtured many superstitious rules: Don't use the word *no-hitter* in the dugout, don't arrange bats in an X, don't step on the foul lines. The men on one minor-league team in Utah, the Salt Lake Trappers, refrained from washing their socks—like the boxer Marvin Johnson, so as not to wash the luck away—throughout a twenty-nine-game winning streak in the summer of 1987. Boston Red Sox third baseman Wade Boggs has developed a detailed routine that occupies him for fully five hours before every home game. In addition to the practical matters of changing into his uniform, warming up his throwing arm, and shagging grounders, his strict private schedule includes precise times for a drink of water and for meditation in center field. It also requires him to finish grounder practice by stepping on third, second, and first bases, in that order; then stepping twice in the first-base coach's box, he goes from there to the dugout in exactly four loping steps.

Taking their cues from the players' clear conviction that magical practices bolster their efforts, sports fans eagerly do their parts with banners, noisemakers, chants, costumes, and their own elaborate spells. One English father and daughter, serious soccer enthusiasts, developed a pregame ritual designed to ensure their hometown team's success. The pair had to take different routes to the stadium, taking care to cross the road only once; then they had to enter by the same turnstile and buy their programs from the same vendor. If either departed from this routine in the slightest way, they both were convinced that the team did not have "a hope in hell."

Although superstition seems to flourish in many situations, is there some pattern in its presence? Researchers who have studied it tend to agree that where danger and uncertainty are high, people tend to be more superstitious. Anthropologist Bronislaw Malinowski developed this theory after he studied fishing practices among Trobriand Islanders. He found that those who fished in a lagoon, where the water was calm and the fish were plentiful, were content to rely on their own skills to bring home enough fish. But those who fished on the open sea, where the waves and reefs could be treacherous and the catch was unpredictable, practiced elaborate magical rituals to ensure their safety and success. Malinowski concluded that people invent magic and ritual to help deal with uncertainty, danger, and fear.

The many superstitions of athletes bear this out. What is more, many coaches and sports experts see this as healthy behavior. "Superstition is a real coping strategy, a way to handle the anxiety that comes with competition," said Graham Neil, a teacher of physical education and sports psychology at Montreal's McGill University. Pregame rituals, other authorities agree, can help athletes prepare for a game, providing a calming sense of control over the unknown. In light of these opinions, it is not surprising that on a football team, the most superstitious players are often the defensive squad—the fellows who play only when the other team controls the ball.

Surely actors, whose success depends not only on the work of many colleagues but on the fickle tastes of crowds of strangers as well, have just as much need for a calming sense of control. Many performers do indeed fill their preperformance moments with painstaking personal rites, taking care, for instance, to wear some lucky piece of clothing or to use only new sticks of makeup on opening nights. The famous team of Alfred Lunt and Lynn Fontanne always

*In hopes of resolving domestic troubles, a
Bangkok woman casts nine live eels into a
canal as a friend observes her offering.
The Thai consider nine a lucky number, and the
setting free of water creatures or birds is a
favored stratagem for changing one's fortunes.*

made sure they arrived in their dressing rooms at least four hours before the curtain and spent the time in relaxed seclusion. Taking the opposite tack, Charles Hawtrey, a star of the English stage early in this century, feared that hanging about the theater would make him nervous and with a superstitious regularity always arranged to leap out of a taxi and dash onstage just in time for his first line.

Sports and theater are by no means the riskiest arenas, of course. People in many other lines of work must place not just their reputations but their lives in the balance as they go about their jobs. Among these are sailors, miners, and airline pilots.

Sailors practice many superstitions to bring good luck in general, and to avoid drowning in particular. They have traditionally endured the tattooist's needle not merely to add decorations to their bodies but to ward off bad luck. A tattoo of a pig or a cockerel on the instep is believed to offer special protection against drowning. The word *pig,* however, must not be spoken on a ship while under way, or bad luck will follow. This may stem from the fact that early sailors, when out of sight of land and uncertain of their bearings, would sometimes pitch a pig overboard, in the belief that the pig would instinctively swim toward land. Even if the unlucky animal was saved from drowning, it would soon enough be slaughtered for food.

Whistling is superstitiously forbidden in many circumstances, because it is said to summon the devil. This malevolent being,

of course, knows what you need and will bring just the opposite or do you in with too much of a good thing. In the heyday of sail, seamen feared that whistling on board ship would "whistle up a wind" and lead to shipwreck. The twin prohibitions against whistling or saying *pig* while on board ship account for a name, The Pig and Whistle, given to many an English waterfront pub—because on land, a sailor can safely do both.

Miners, like sailors, also avoid whistling while they work, lest they displease the "knockers," the irritable underground spirits who can arrange cave-ins. Generations of Welsh miners have superstitiously avoided washing their backs, for fear that the knockers would spitefully bring down a mineshaft ceiling to soil a clean back. Ever watchful for omens, British miners walking to work might turn back and go home if they passed a cross-eyed person, and if that omen did not deter them, a dove or a robin near the mineshaft might.

Among people who pursue hazardous occupations of recent vintage, airplane pilots are especially prone to carry lucky rabbits' feet; some insist that the seatbelts in unoccupied seats be fastened before takeoff; and many pilots and crew members take care not to utter the word *crash* before or during a flight. In the same spirit, many automobile owners carefully avoid saying the word *accident.* Professional racecar driver Mario Andretti scrupulously avoided the color green in all of his clothing and equipment.

Gamblers, whose pastime

is chance itself, have lots of superstitions. The expression "playing a hunch" refers to the old belief that it was lucky to touch a hunchback's hump before placing a bet. Many bingo players rely on what they consider their lucky cards and their lucky seat. A poker player suffering a run of losing cards might ask for a new deck or change seats or simply turn the chair around—or even get up and walk counterclockwise around the chair three times and sit back down. Another remedy for bad cards is to spread a handkerchief on the chair, then sit on it. Some players think that laying two used matches in an X in an ashtray will cross out their opponents' luck. And gamblers are careful not to boast or sing or lend money to other gamblers, so as not to lose any of their good fortune.

Uncertainties, of course, are plentiful, not just in work but in everyday life. The hazards of the unknown seem to multiply, however, at the times of life's transitions—birth, courtship, marriage, illness, and death. Not surprisingly, superstitions have sprung up around each of these tricky passages.

In many countries, planting an apple tree when a child is born is said to ensure a fruitful and prosperous life for both. Certain other birth beliefs are not so sanguine: According to some rural Americans, anyone born during a thunderstorm will eventually die by lightning, and if a baby's first diaper is an old one, the child will grow up to be a thief. On the other hand, if a newborn's first journey is upstairs, a lifetime of high-minded pursuits is guaranteed. Some people offer an infant a choice between a silver dollar, a deck of playing cards, and a Bible; the child's choice, they say, foretells its profession—as a banker, gambler, or preacher. The same people might avoid stepping over a baby so as not to stunt its growth.

In the matter of choosing a mate, superstition is far from silent. Many cultures offer a young unmarried woman various magical means by which to conjure a clue to her future husband's identity. In the Ozarks, she may hang her kerchief from a bush on the night before May Day, in hopes that her future husband's initials will appear in dew on the cloth the next morning. Another tradition tells her to go at dawn to a spring, carrying an egg in a glass; when she pours water into the glass, she may capture a vision of her husband to be—and even the children to come. In the days when a bride always took her husband's surname, a woman was cautioned to choose a mate whose last initial was different from hers: "Change the name and not the letter, change for worse and not for better."

Many brides follow an old custom in making sure to wear "something old, something new, something borrowed, and something blue" on their wedding day. The old item should be one that has been lucky before; the new is for hope, the borrowed carries a well-wisher's good luck, and the blue is expected to banish evil spirits from the day and from the couple's married life. After the wedding, a tradition-minded groom may carry his bride over the threshold into their new home. Some say this is to prevent a stumble on her part, which would augur badly for their life together. Others speculate that the practice goes back to early European barbarian tribesmen, who forcibly kidnapped the women they wished to wed and who could get them into their huts by no other means.

A number of widespread folk beliefs deal with sickness, medicine, and healing. In the Ozarks, a pickle placed in the mouth of a newborn is expected to ward off colic. Countryfolk also claim that putting the tip of a cat's tail up a child's nose will cure a nosebleed. Among the many cures for a wart is this complex one: Steal a piece of meat, rub it on the wart, then bury it where rainwater drips from the eaves; as the meat rots, the wart will disappear.

Black, the color of mourning in Western countries,

Wizardry in a Candle's Flame

Ever since hunter-gatherers discovered how to nurse flames to life, dispersing the darkness of night and chasing the chill away, humankind has been fascinated by the power of fire. Ancient tribes danced and chanted around campfires in hopes of invoking unseen spirits. In time, legends linked fire with the gods. In Greek mythology, for instance, fire belonged to the gods alone until Prometheus stole the sacred flame and gave it to humans. To this day, many of the world's religions associate fire with divinity: Christianity, Judaism, and Hinduism, for example, all observe candle-lighting ceremonies.

Symbolic of change, purification, and sacrifice, fire has long been a magician's tool as well. Indeed, a whole branch of occult lore has grown around the use of candles. Through the ritual burning of a candle whose color is mystically related to certain characteristics, adepts say, one's innermost desires can be fulfilled.

In general, candle ceremonies are easy to perform and require little equipment—just simple candleholders and the candles themselves. Selena Fox, a priestess in the present-day nature religion of Wicca, tells people to first choose the candle colors that represent their goals. Her guidelines for color selection appear on the next page—a gold candle for financial rewards, for example, a pink one for romance—but there are no strict rules. If someone feels green suggests money more strongly than gold does, it can be used instead. And several candles may be burned at once for multiple wishes. Ordinary tapers will do, although some people prefer specially shaped candles signifying their goals—human images for personal relationships, hearts for love, and so on.

The ceremony should be done at a peaceful site where candles can be safely burned, away from curtains and upholstery. They should not be left burning unattended; it is wise to keep water or a fire extinguisher nearby.

Mystics say candle magic works best when the moon is full. Many candle burners symbolically cleanse themselves first by bathing. Some use incense to enhance the aura of spirituality. They prepare for the rite by trying to rid their minds of extraneous thoughts, focusing instead on their goals. Fox tells them to start by asking for the blessing and guidance of whatever spiritual power or deity they venerate, then lighting the candle. Participants should repeat the following chant three times: "Sacred candle, sacred flame, aid the magic that I name." Then, she says, for at least five minutes they should repeat an appropriate chant from the next page, each keyed for use with a candle color. A few words of thanksgiving should be said before the the flame is extinguished and the ceremony concluded.

Red
For vitality, passion, and creativity

Vitality! Vitality! Vitality!
Power of passion, rise up in me!

Orange
For assertiveness and endurance

I assert my power to overcome obstacles!
I assert my power to get my needs fulfilled!

Yellow
For happiness, success, and self-esteem

Happiness and success,
come to me.
I deserve you!

Green
For health and nurturing love

Good health and love that nurtures,
Come to me and my environment!

Blue
For inner peace and friendship

Serenity, serenity, serenity.
Peace be within me
and around me.

Indigo
For deep relaxation and restful sleep

Stress, be gone!
Relaxation, come.

Purple
For inner power and spiritual mastery

Divine power within me,
Bless me and guide me on the
path of my destiny.

Gold
For wealth and generosity

Money, wealth, power of plenty,
come to me,
So I can get richer and be more
generous to others.

Silver
For intuition and dreams

Insights, dreams, and intuitions,
come to me, and
Bless me with inner wisdom and
self-understanding.

White
For purification, protection, and unity

I am purified. I am protected.
I am one with the radiant
white light of
divine wholesomeness.

Black
For change, release, and renewal

Power of change, you are
within me!
Awaken my powers of
choice and freedom! And
release me from bondage to
harmful addictions!

Brown
To center oneself, for security and comfort

I am becoming more centered,
more comfortable
and more secure within
myself and my home.

Pink
For romance and love

Power of loving partnership
come to me.
Heal any breaks in my heart
from the past and
Guide my choices in intimacy in
the present and future.

Rainbow
For harmony, balance, and community

Harmony! Harmony! Harmony!
Balance within me and the circle
of life that includes me!

was originally intended to make survivors invisible to the spirit that had claimed the deceased and that was thought to linger around the body, looking for more victims. Similarly, coins laid on the eyelids of corpses were meant to keep the dead from looking around for others to join them in death. To the superstitious, death announces its coming through many signs. The cry of a whippoorwill or the hoot of an owl is to many people a death omen. If a house dog sleeps with his paws beneath him, according to one belief, then news of death is approaching from the direction in which his tail points. Scottish Highlanders share with many other rural folk a belief that carrying a spade or other digging tool into a house through the front door brings death—presumably because such tools can be used to dig graves. Although superstitions settle thickly around life's milestones, everyday life is also rich with omens and precautions. Ordinary clothing, for instance, provides plenty of opportunities for superstitious behavior. In Hungary, it is considered bad luck to mend clothing while the owner is wearing it, lest the devil mistake the garment for a shroud and claim the soul. A prudent mother might give her child a piece of thread to chew on, to show he is alive, while she stitches up his torn shirt. In France, any article of clothing inadvertently put on inside out is good luck, but it must be worn that way all day if the luck is to hold. In England, a button or hook fastened the wrong way invites bad luck; the peril can be reversed, however, by undoing all the fasteners and starting the job over. Superstitious English folk also believe that picking up one's own glove after dropping it brings bad luck, whereas a glove that has been dropped by one person and retrieved by another assures good fortune for both.

It is bad luck—a portent of death, in fact—to put shoes on a table in England. In Italy, the same meaning attaches to a hat on a bed. The popular American entertainer Jimmy Durante, a son of Italian immigrants, had a strong fear of this omen. Fortunately, he also had an antidote; he believed he could avert the ill omen of a hat on the bed by immediately hanging up the offending hat and then not touching it again until he was wearing another hat. Some of his friends, familiar with the ins and outs of this ritual, once decided to catch him up in its toils. They bought twenty-five dime-store hats and scattered them on his bed, then hid in the bathroom to await developments. When Durante discovered the hats, his careful ceremonies to reverse the bad luck kept the conspirators entertained for quite some time.

All sorts of portents may be read in shudders, coughs, and sneezes. In Scotland, a baby's first sneeze is said to release the child from the power of the fairies. Someone who sneezes while speaking, an American belief holds, is thereby shown to be telling the truth, while a coughing fit proves that the victim has been lying. A sudden shiver is said in England and the United States to mean that somebody has just walked over what will one day be the shiverer's grave.

Preserved in many rural beliefs is the notion that omens found in ordinary life—such as the movements of clouds and the actions of animals—can tell the future, to those who know how to read them. A cat washing itself in a doorway, for instance, may be interpreted in the Midwest as portending a clergyman's visit to the house, and if a rooster crows before midnight, some say, a change in weather is on the way. Other superstitions tell how to avoid dangers lurking around the home. A tree that has been struck by lightning must never be used for firewood, countryfolk in western Wisconsin say, for it will draw lightning to the house. Anyone who sweeps dirt out the door of a house is believed by some southern blacks to sweep the luck out along with it; the prudent method is to collect the refuse in the middle of the floor, pick it up, and carry it out.

In many rural areas, the problem of getting water out of the ground—a project at once essential and laced with uncertainties—lends itself to many magical and superstitious practices. The most common of these is witching, or dowsing, with a forked stick; it is performed in most parts of the world, including the United States. Using both hands to hold the stick's two branches, the dowser walks around with the third point extended and waits for it to dip down, seemingly of its own volition, thus indicating the presence of a subterranean spring. Despite the efforts of physical scientists to brand the practice a foolish superstition, dowsing for water has persisted.

Since the practice was so widespread, two social scientists—psychologist Ray Hyman and anthropologist Evon Z. Vogt—undertook in 1966 to study it. Building on Malinowski's observation that magic multiplies where fear and uncertainty are greatest, they developed a theory about American water witching and then set out to test it. Their guess was that the harder it was to predict where water could be found in an area, the more water witches would be working that territory.

The two researchers first selected a range of counties, based on United States Geological Survey records of the difficulty of finding water in them, then consulted with those counties' agricultural extension agents, asking how many water witches were known in their areas. The results upheld their theory: Where geologists' predictions of water were least accurate, there the dowsers were most abundant. Noting that "magic serves an important function," Hyman and Vogt called witching "a ritual that reduces anxiety." In other words, many people preferred to walk around watching the dowser dowse, rather than sit around worrying and feeling helpless.

But the fact is, dowsers do sometimes find water. Perhaps the explanation is that a so-called water witch, walking around and looking at a limited area year after year, sometimes finding water and sometimes finding none, may absorb a kind of visceral sense of where water is likely to be in that county. Geologists, meanwhile, are stuck with broad general principles. In some places, if the dowsers actually come up with more water, it is because at least they try. Water witching persists because it works. And the fact that it works, at least sometimes, brings dowsing squarely into the debate between magic and science, the ongoing quest to pin down the line that is supposed to divide superstition from reason.

It sometimes happens that new information—an invention or discovery—moves a phenomenon across that elusive dividing line and converts it from superstition to science. The idea that people could fly was, in the age of witches, dismissed as mere superstitious delusion. Now, in the jet and

In the village of Gende in northwest Spain, three women balancing second heads made of wax attend an outdoor mass in a Trinity Sunday ceremony that mixes ancient magical traditions with Catholicism. The replicas signify their hopes for relief from depression or an illness of the head—mental or physical. Other worshipers taking part may sport arms, legs, or hearts of wax, depending on their afflictions. When the mass is over, the wax body parts are laid before a shrine.

rocket age, flying has become science. Edward Jenner, the eighteenth-century English physician who discovered vaccination, based his revolutionary scientific work on a folk belief, a superstition, of his native Gloucestershire.

Local opinion held that a person who had been infected with cowpox, a relatively harmless infection caught from cattle, was thereafter immune to the much more deadly ailment of human smallpox. Jenner's medical contemporaries disregarded this notion, but Jenner wondered if there was anything to it. Working at first in secret, to avoid his colleagues' derision, he carried out his experiments. Eventually his investigations led to the discovery of vaccination—the method of introducing a minor, relatively harmless infection into the human body so as to render it immune to more serious disease. His method demonstrated the truth of his new theory of infection and immunity and became a pillar of modern medicine.

Most superstitions, of course, have no scientifically provable efficacy, and many modern people cling to customs that they would never try to tie to science. Superstitious pursuits and invocations of magic—from dowsing for water, to carrying lucky charms, to tossing spilled salt— show a human willingness to believe, a faith in magic, which has its roots in childhood. At a certain age—usually between four and eleven—children all over the world, in all sorts of cultures, go through a developmental stage when their thinking is magical. The Swiss psychologist Jean Piaget discovered that what young children believe about space, time, and why things happen is fundamentally different from what adults believe.

Piaget found that young children think that a ball of clay, rolled out into a snake shape, has somehow been made into a smaller amount of clay. They cannot say how, but they believe it "just happens"; lack of an explanation does not defeat belief. Piaget's studies convinced him that very young children, free from the demands of reason, do not naturally see any border between psychological events and physical phenomena. Instead they feel that they can cause events, or make things change, by looking at them, by thinking about them, by wishing. The very young perceive no difference, and no border, between themselves and things. Trees and stones, to a very young child, have spirits and minds too, and dreams are just as real as waking events. Thus children are free to believe with all their hearts in Santa Claus, the tooth fairy, and other logically impossible incorporeal beings. Children, among themselves and

away from adult explanations and theories, seem to possess their own child culture and to hand on their magical beliefs.

One of the universal superstitions of childhood is heard in the rhyme, "Step on a crack, break your mother's back." Such a belief may at first glance seem independent of adult culture. But the belief does not always die with childhood; no less an intellectual giant than Dr. Samuel Johnson, the eighteenth-century dictionary writer, avoided stepping on cracks all his life, and so too does actress Claire Bloom. All superstitions—from the evil eye to the avoidance of cracks—partake of magical thinking. Many survive all argument, proof, and experience to the contrary—all the weapons of rationality and adulthood. In many adults, childhood superstitions may soften to a kind of half belief, so that an educated big-city businessman might laugh at himself for always putting on his right sock and his right shoe first; but he still does it, just in case. Superstitions, fruits of the vine of magical belief, live on because that vine is so deeply rooted in the fertile soil of childhood.

Ironically enough, twentieth-century science has argued persuasively for the permanence and even the usefulness of pure superstition. Margaret Mead, the pioneering anthropologist, observed that "superstition has been a part of every civilization's culture." Coaches who say superstition is valuable to players in competition are not the only people who conclude it has a place in the modern psyche.

Authorities in human behavior contend superstitious beliefs may actually reduce stress and enhance survival.

Clifford Swensen, a professor of psychology at Purdue University, acknowledges that "superstition is a primitive way of coping with life. In trying to control every aspect of their lives, people subscribe to certain rituals even though they have no logical connection with the future." However, despite their illogic, Swensen too believes that such practices can have a positive effect: "If you believe a certain ritual will help you reach a goal, it may influence you in ways that will help you achieve your aim. Wearing a 'lucky' necklace, for instance, may make you feel more optimistic and could result in a more positive mental approach." In other words, people persist in their superstitions because, like water witching, they sometimes work. Superstitions provide the sense that a person can take powerful action to gain control of a situation. Such feelings of power are valuable and can bolster self-confidence. They help people everywhere, despite real uncertainties and dangers, to find the strength to get on with the everyday business of life.

Many superstitions engender a sense of control by a sort of two-way structure: They carry with them a prescribed antidote that can be used by believers who accidentally invite ill fortune. A person who breaks a mirror may banish the bad luck by dropping the pieces into a flowing stream or by covering the shards with a five-dollar bill and making the sign of the cross. Tossing spilled salt in the prescribed manner is supposed to avert the expected trouble. Even the longstanding and dreaded curse of Macbeth has its counterspell.

Many a novice actor has learned of the curse from older colleagues only after accidentally invoking it by quoting from the play offstage. Fortunately, the veterans usually know how to avert catastrophe. The offender is instructed to leave the room, turn around three times, spit, knock on the door three times, and beg very humbly to be allowed back in. The simple ritual will effectively neutralize the curse and restore safety. In this situation, at least, fate is highly forgiving.

ACKNOWLEDGMENTS

The editors would like to thank the following for their assistance in the preparation of this volume.

François Avril, Conservateur, Département des Manuscrits, Bibliothèque Nationale, Paris; Professor Hans Bender, Institut für Grenzgebiete der Psychologie und Psychohygiene, Freiburg, West Germany; Carol Edwards, Department of Egyptian Antiquities, British Museum, London; Nat Edwards, Department of Mediaeval Antiquities, British Museum, London; Russell Feather, Smithsonian Institution, Washington, D.C.; Dr. Nina Gockerell, Bayerisches Nationalmuseum, Munich, West Germany; Michael Holford, Loughton, England; Dr. Rudolf Kaschewsky, Zentralasiatisches Institut, Universität Bonn, West Germany; John King, Buffalo Gallery, Alexandria, Virginia; Pam King, Buffalo Gallery, Alexandria, Virginia; Heidi Klein, Bildarchiv Preussischer Kulturbesitz, West Berlin; Gabrielle Kohler, Archiv für Kunst und Geschichte, West Berlin; Adalgisa Lugli, Turin, Italy; Dr. Hermann Maué, Germanisches Nationalmuseum, Nuremberg, West Germany; Robert Moes, Brooklyn; Hans Roth, Zentralasiatisches Institut, Universität Bonn, West Germany; Brian Shuel, London; Rolf Streichardt, Institut für Grenzgebiete der Psychologie und Psychohygiene, Freiburg, West Germany.

PICTURE CREDITS

BIBLIOGRAPHY

Alderman, Clifford Lindsey, *Symbols of Magic: Amulets and Talismans*. New York: Julian Messner, 1977.
Andrews, Carol, ed., *The Ancient Egyptian Book of the Dead*. Transl. by Raymond O. Faulkner. London: British Museum, 1985.
Binder, Pearl, *Magic Symbols of the World*. London: Hamlyn, 1973.
Blair, Lawrence, with Lorne Blair, *Ring of Fire*. Toronto: Bantam Books, 1988.
Blakeslee, Sandra, "Folklore Mirrors Life's Key Themes." *New York Times*, August 14, 1985.
Blofeld, John, and the Editors of Time-Life Books, *Bangkok* (The Great Cities series). Amsterdam: Time-Life Books, 1979.
Blum, Ralph, *The Book of Runes*. New York: Oracle Books, 1987.
Bord, Janet, and Colin Bord:
Ancient Mysteries of Britain. Manchester, N.H.: Salem House, 1986.
Mysterious Britain. London: Granada, 1974.
Bowness, Charles, *Romany Magic*. Wellingborough, Northamptonshire, England: Aquarian Press, 1973.
Bridaham, Lester Burbank, *Gargoyles, Chimeres, and the Grotesque in French Gothic Sculpture*. New York: Architectural Book, 1930.
Brown, Michael F., *Tsewa's Gift: Magic and Meaning in an Amazonian Society*. Washington, D.C.: Smithsonian Institution Press, 1986.
Buckland, Ray, ed., *Llewellyn's 1990 Magickal Almanac*. St. Paul: Llewellyn Publications, 1989.
Budge, E. A. Wallis, *Amulets and Superstitions*. New York: Dover, 1978 (reprint of 1930 edition).
Capps, Benjamin, and the Editors of Time-Life Books, *The Indians* (The Old West series). New York: Time-Life Books, 1973.
Carroll, David, *The Magic Makers*. New York: Arbor House, 1974.
Carroll, David, and Barry Saxe, *Natural Magic: The Magical State of Being*. New York: Arbor House, 1977.
Cavendish, Richard:
The Black Arts. New York: G. P. Putnam's Sons, 1967.
A History of Magic. London: Weidenfeld & Nicolson, 1977.
Cavendish, Richard, ed.:
Encyclopedia of the Unexplained. London: Routledge & Kegan Paul, 1974.
Man, Myth & Magic. New York: Marshall Cavendish, 1985.
Claypoole, John P., *Johnny Claypoole, Hexologist*. Lenhartsville, Pa.: Privately published, 1987.
Colton, Harold S., *Hopi Kachina Dolls: With a Key to Their*

Identification. Albuquerque, N.M.: University of New Mexico Press, 1959.

Conn, Richard, *Circles of the World: Traditional Art of the Plains Indians* (exhibition catalog). Denver: Denver Art Museum, 1982.

Connell, Evan S., *Son of the Morning Star: Custer and the Little Bighorn.* New York: Harper & Row, 1985.

Conway, David, *Magic: An Occult Primer.* New York: E. P. Dutton, 1972.

Courlander, Harold, *The Fourth World of the Hopis.* Greenwich, Conn.: Fawcett, 1972.

Coze, Paul, "Kachinas: Masked Dancers of the Southwest." *National Geographic Magazine,* August 1957.

Crossley-Holland, Kevin, ed., *The Norse Myths.* New York: Random House, 1980.

Davis, Wade, *The Serpent and the Rainbow.* London: Collins, 1986.

Denning, Melita, and Osborne Phillips:
Magical States of Consciousness. St. Paul: Llewellyn Publications, 1985.
Voudoun Fire: The Living Reality of Mystical Religion. St. Paul: Llewellyn Publications, 1979.

Drury, Nevill, *The Path of the Chameleon.* Jersey, Channel Islands, England: Neville Spearman, 1973.

Eliade, Mircea, *Shamanism: Archaic Techniques of Ecstasy.* Transl. by Willard R. Trask. Princeton, N.J.: Princeton University Press, 1964.

Elworthy, Frederick Thomas, *The Evil Eye: An Account of This Ancient and Widespread Superstition.* New York: Julian Press, 1986.

Erdoes, Richard, *The Sun Dance People: The Plains Indians, Their Past and Present.* New York: Alfred A. Knopf, 1972.

Farren, David, *The Return of Magic.* New York: Harper & Row, 1972.

Fisher, Marc, "Dr. Buzzard's Voodoo Cure." *Washington Post Magazine,* December 11, 1988.

Fitzhugh, William W., and Aron Crowell, *Crossroads of Continents: Cultures of Siberia and Alaska.* Washington, D.C.: Smithsonian Institution Press, 1988.

Gandolfo, Charles Massicot, *Voodoo in South Louisiana.* New Orleans: New Orleans Historic Voodoo Museum, 1987.

Goldstein, Steve, "Superstitious? Naah!" *World Tennis,* February 1985.

González-Wippler, Migene, *The Complete Book of Spells, Ceremonies and Magic.* St. Paul: Llewellyn Publications, 1988.

Green, Marian, *The Gentle Arts of Aquarian Magic.* Wellingborough, Northamptonshire, England: Aquarian Press, 1987.

Gregor, Arthur S., *Amulets, Talismans, and Fetishes.* New York: Charles Scribner's Sons, 1975.

Greub, Suzanne, ed., *Expressions of Belief: Masterpieces of African, Oceanic, and Indonesian Art* (exhibition catalog). New York: Rizzoli International Publications, 1988.

Haberman, Clyde, "Modern Japan, Land of Superstition." *New York Times,* July 12, 1986.

Haining, Peter, *Superstitions.* London: Sidgwick and Jackson, 1979.

Haislip, Barbara, *Stars, Spells, Secrets and Sorcery: A Do-It-Yourself Book of the Occult.* Boston: Little, Brown, 1976.

Halifax, Joan, *Shaman: The Wounded Healer.* New York: Crossroad, 1982.

Hansmann, Liselotte, and Lenz Kriss-Rettenbeck, *Amulett und Talisman.* Munich: Georg D. W. Callwey, 1966.

Hawthorn, Audrey, *Kwakiutl Art.* Seattle: University of Washington Press, 1979.

Highwater, Jamake, *Ritual of the Wind: North American Indian Ceremonies, Music, and Dance.* New York: Alfred Van Der Marck Editions, 1984.

Holroyd, Stuart, and Neil Powell, *Mysteries of Magic.* London: Aldus Books, 1978.

Howes, Michael, *Amulets.* London: Robert Hale, 1975.

Huggett, Richard:
The Curse of Macbeth and Other Theatrical Superstitions. Chippenham, Wiltshire, England: Picton, 1981.
Supernatural on Stage: Ghosts and Superstitions of the Theatre. New York: Taplinger, 1975.

Index to Occult Sciences (A New Library of the Supernatural). Garden City, N.Y.: Doubleday, 1977.

Ions, Veronica, *Egyptian Mythology.* New York: Peter Bedrick Books, 1988.

Jahoda, Gustav, *The Psychology of Superstition.* Baltimore: Penguin Books, 1969.

Jonaitis, Aldona, *From the Land of the Totem Poles.* New York: American Museum of Natural History, 1988.

Kay, Linda, "A Little Bit of Voodoo." *Women's Sports and Fitness,* June 1986.

Keller, Bill, "The Russians, Too, Embrace 'Secret Silliness' of Astrology." *New York Times,* May 14, 1988.

Kerr, Howard, and Charles L. Crow, eds., *The Occult in America: New Historical Perspectives.* Urbana, Ill.: University of Illinois Press, 1983.

King, Francis, *Ritual Magic in England: 1887 to the Present Day.* London: Neville Spearman, 1970.

King, Francis X., *Witchcraft and Demonology.* New York: Exeter Books, 1987.

King, Serge, *Kahuna Healing: Holistic Health and Healing Practices of Polynesia.* Wheaton, Ill.: The Theosophical Publishing House, 1983.

Lippman, Deborah, and Paul Colin, *How to Make Amulets, Charms and Talismans: What They Mean and How to Use Them.* New York: M. Evans, 1974.

Logan, Jo, *The Prediction Book of Amulets and Talismans.* Poole, Dorset, England: Javelin Books, 1986.

Lurker, Manfred, *The Gods and Symbols of Ancient Egypt.* Transl. by Barbara Cummings. New York: Thames and Hudson, 1980.

McCallum, Jack, "Green Cats, Black Cats and Lady Luck." *Sports Illustrated,* February 8, 1988.

MacCulloch, J. A., *The Religion of the Ancient Celts.* Edinburgh, Scotland: T. & T. Clark, 1911.

McGuire, Harriet C., "Woyo Pot Lids." *African Arts,* February 1980.

Maloney, Clarence, ed., *The Evil Eye.* New York: Columbia University Press, 1976.

Maple, Eric, *Superstition and the Superstitious.* New York: A. S. Barnes, 1972.

Mathers, S. Liddell MacGregor, transl. and ed., *The Key of Solomon the King.* New Beach, Me.: Samuel Weiser, 1974.

Mauss, Marcel, *A General Theory of Magic.* Transl. by Robert Brain. London: Routledge & Kegan Paul, 1972.

Mercatante, Anthony S., *The Facts on File Encyclopedia of World Mythology and Legend.* New York: Facts on File, 1988.

Métraux, Alfred, *Voodoo in Haiti.* Transl. by Hugo Charteris. New York: Schocken Books, 1972.

Michell, John, *The Earth Spirit: Its Ways, Shrines and Mysteries.* London: Avon, 1975.

Moes, Robert, *Auspicious Spirits: Korean Folk Paintings and Related Objects* (exhibition catalog). Washington, D.C.: International Exhibitions Foundation, 1983.

Morrill, Sibley S., comp. and ed., *The Kahunas: The Black—and White—Magicians of Hawaii.* Boston: Branden Press, 1969.

National Geographic Society:
Discovering Britain & Ireland. Washington, D.C.: National Geographic Society, 1985.
The World of the American Indian. Washington, D.C.: National Geographic Society, 1979.

Nemy, Enid, "New Yorkers, etc." *New York Times,* November 8, 1987.

Newall, Venetia, *The Encyclopedia of Witchcraft & Magic.* New York: Dial Press, 1974.

Nicholson, Shirley, comp., *Shamanism: An Expanded View of Reality.* Wheaton, Ill.: Theosophical Publishing House, 1987.

O'Keefe, Daniel Lawrence, *Stolen Lightning: The Social Theory of Magic.* New York: Random House, 1982.

Opie, Iona, and Moira Tatem, eds., *A Dictionary of Superstitions.* Oxford, England: Oxford University Press, 1989.

Page, Jake, "Inside the Sacred Hopi Homeland." *National Geographic,* November 1982.

Page, Michael, and Robert Ingpen, *Encyclopedia of Things That Never Were: Creatures, Places, and People.* New York: Viking Penguin, 1987.

Parsons, Anne, *Belief, Magic, and Anomie.* London: Collier-Macmillan, 1969.

Perl, Lila, *Don't Sing Before Breakfast, Don't Sleep in the Moonlight: Everyday Superstitions and How They Began.* New York: Ticknor & Fields, 1988.

Podmore, Frank, *Mediums of the 19th Century.* Vol. 2. New Hyde Park, N.Y.: University Books, 1963.

Pogrebin, Letty Cottin, "Superstitious Minds." *MS.,* February 1988.

Rachleff, Owen S. *The Secrets of Superstitions: How They Help, How They Hurt.* Garden City, N.Y.: Doubleday, 1976.

Radford, E., and M. A. Radford, *Encyclopaedia of Superstitions.* Westport, Conn.: Greenwood Press, 1969 (reprint of 1949 edition).

The Rand McNally Atlas of the Body and Mind. New York: Rand McNally, 1976.

Reynolds, Barrie, *Magic, Divination and Witchcraft among the Barotse of Northern Rhodesia.* Los Angeles: University of California Press, 1963.

Rigaud, Milo, *Secrets of Voodoo.* Transl. by Robert B. Cross. New York: Arco, 1969.

Rodman, Julius Scammon, *The Kahuna Sorcerers of Hawaii, Past and Present.* Hicksville, N.Y.: Exposition Press, 1979.

Rubin, F., *Learning and Sleep: The Theory and Practice of Hypnopaedia.* Bristol, England: John Wright & Sons, 1971.

Russell, Jeffrey B., *A History of Witchcraft: Sorcerers, Heretics, and Pagans.* London: Thames and Hudson, 1980.

Ryback, David, with Letitia Sweitzer, *Dreams That Come True: Their Psychic and Transforming Powers.* New York: Bantam, 1988.

Schlich, Kim, and Victor Schlich, "Me? Superstitious?" *Seventeen,* October 1985.

Seabrook, W. B., *The Magic Island.* New York: Paragon House, 1989 (reprint of 1929 edition).

Seligmann, Kurt, *Magic, Supernaturalism and Religion.* London: Allen Lane, 1971.

Shepard, Leslie, ed., *Encyclopedia of Occultism & Parapsychology.* Vol. 1. Detroit: Gale Research, 1984.

Sheridan, Ronald, and Anne Ross, *Gargoyles and Grotesques: Paganism in the Medieval Church.* Boston: New York Graphic Society, 1975.

Skelton, Robin, *Talismanic Magic.* York Beach, Me.: Samuel

Weiser, 1985.

Smith, Robert T., *Cult & Occult*. Minneapolis: Winston Press, 1973.

Steiger, Brad, *American Indian Magic: Sacred Pow Wows and Hopi Prophecies*. New Brunswick, N.J.: Inner Light Publications, 1986.

Tallant, Robert, *Voodoo in New Orleans*. Gretna, La.: Pelican, 1983 (reprint of 1946 edition).

Thomas, Keith, *Religion and the Decline of Magic*. New York: Charles Scribner's Sons, 1971.

Thompson, C. J. S.:
The Hand of Destiny: Folklore and Superstition for Everyday Life. New York: Bell, 1989 (reprint of 1932 edition).
The Mysteries and Secrets of Magic. Detroit: Singing Tree Press, 1971 (reprint of 1928 edition).

Thompson, Robert Farris, *Flash of the Spirit*. New York: Random House, 1983.

Thorsson, Edred, *Futhark: A Handbook of Rune Magic*. York Beach, Me.: Samuel Weiser, 1984.

Tuleja, Tad, *Curious Customs: The Stories behind 296 Popular American Rituals*. New York: Crown, 1987.

Underhill, Ruth M., *Red Man's Religion: Beliefs and Practices of the Indians North of Mexico*. Chicago: University of Chicago Press, 1965.

Vinci, Leo, *Talismans, Amulets and Charms*. London: Regency Press, 1977.

Volavkova, Zdenka, "Nkisi Figures of the Lower Congo." *African Arts*, winter 1972.

"Voodoo: The Harvard-Haiti Connection." *Discover*, January 1989.

Waite, Arthur Edward, *Alchemists through the Ages*. New York: Rudolf Steiner, 1970 (reprint of 1888 edition).

Waters, Frank, *Book of the Hopi*. New York: Viking Press, 1963.

Weatherford, Jack, *Indian Givers: How the Indians of the Americas Transformed the World*. New York: Crown, 1988.

Welfare, Simon, and John Fairley, *Arthur C. Clarke's Mysterious World*. New York: A & W, 1980.

Westermarck, Edward, *Pagan Survivals in Mohammedan Civilisation*. Amsterdam: Philo Press, 1973 (reprint of 1933 edition).

Westwood, Jennifer, ed., *The Atlas of Mysterious Places*. New York: Weidenfeld & Nicolson, 1987.

Woodcock, George, *Peoples of the Coast: The Indians of the Pacific Northwest*. Bloomington, Ind.: Indiana University Press, 1977.

Wright, Barton:
Hopi Kachinas: The Complete Guide to Collecting Kachina Dolls. Flagstaff, Ariz.: Northland Press, 1977.
Kachinas: A Hopi Artist's Documentary. Flagstaff, Ariz.: Northland Press with the Heard Museum, Phoenix, 1973.

Zimmer, Judith, "Courting the Gods of Sport." *Psychology Today*, July 1984.

INDEX

Time-Life Books Inc.
is a wholly owned subsidiary of
THE TIME INC. BOOK COMPANY

President and Chief Executive Officer: Kelso F. Sutton
President, Time Inc. Books Direct: Christopher T. Linen

TIME-LIFE BOOKS INC.

EDITOR: George Constable
Director of Design: Louis Klein
Director of Editorial Resources: Phyllis K. Wise
Director of Photography and Research: John Conrad Weiser

PRESIDENT: John M. Fahey, Jr.
Senior Vice Presidents: Robert M. DeSena, Paul R. Stewart,
Curtis G. Viebranz, Joseph J. Ward
Vice Presidents: Stephen L. Bair, Bonita L. Boezeman, Mary
P. Donohoe, Stephen L. Goldstein, Juanita T. James, An-
drew P. Kaplan, Trevor Lunn, Susan J. Maruyama, Robert
H. Smith
New Product Development: Trevor Lunn, Donia Ann Steele
Supervisor of Quality Control: James King

PUBLISHER: Joseph J. Ward

Editorial Operations
Production: Celia Beattie
Library: Louise D. Forstall
Computer Composition: Gordon E. Buck (Manager),
Deborah G. Tait, Monika D. Thayer, Janet Barnes Syring,
Lillian Daniels

Library of Congress Cataloging in Publication Data
Magical Arts by the editors of Time-Life Books.
    p. cm.—(Mysteries of the unknown.)
    Includes bibliographical references.
    ISBN 0-8094-6380-6   ISBN 0-8094-6381-4 (lib. bdg.)
    1. Magic   2. Magic—History   I. Time-Life Books.
    II. Series.
    BF1611.M374 199081-4   90-31509
    133.4'3—dc20   CIP

MYSTERIES OF THE UNKNOWN

SERIES DIRECTOR: Jim Hicks
Series Administrator: Myrna Traylor-Herndon
Designers: Herbert H. Quarmby, Christopher M. Register

Editorial Staff for *Magical Arts*
Associate Editors: Susan V. Kelly (pictures); Robert A.
Doyle (text)
Text Editors: Dale M. Brown, Janet Cave
Researchers: Patti H. Cass, Sarah D. Ince, Christian D.
Kinney, Elizabeth Ward
Staff Writers: Marfé Ferguson Delano, Margery A. duMond
Assistant Designer: Susan M. Gibas
Copy Coordinators: Mary Beth Oelkers-Keegan, Colette
Stockum
Picture Coordinator: Leanne G. Miller
Editorial Assistant: Donna Fountain

Special Contributors: Lesley Coleman (London, picture
research); Susan Yang K. Chew (lead research); Sheila
Green, Philip M. Murphy, Patricia A. Paterno, Evelyn S.
Prettyman, (research); George Daniels, Betty De Ramus,
Norman Draper, Selena Fox, Gus Hedberg, Anna Cifelli
Isgro, Alison Kahn, John I. Merritt, Wendy Murphy, Peter
Pocock, James Schutze (text); John Drummond (design);
Hazel Blumberg-McKee (index).

Correspondents: Elisabeth Kraemer-Singh (Bonn), Christina
Lieberman (New York), Maria Vincenza Aloisi (Paris), Ann
Natanson (Rome).
Valuable assistance was also provided by Angelika Lem-
mer (Bonn); Judy Aspinall, Christine Hinze (London); Trini
Bandrès (Madrid); Elizabeth Brown (New York); Ann Wise
(Rome); K. C. Hwang (Seoul); Traudl Lessing (Vienna).

Consultants:
Marcello Truzzi, general consultant for the series, is a
professor of sociology at Eastern Michigan University. He
is also director of the Center for Scientific Anomalies
Research (CSAR) and editor of its journal, the *Zetetic
Scholar*. Dr. Truzzi, who considers himself a "constructive
skeptic" with regard to claims of the paranormal, works
through the CSAR to produce dialogues between critics
and proponents of unusual scientific claims.

Other Publications:

AMERICAN COUNTRY
THE THIRD REICH
VOYAGE THROUGH THE UNIVERSE
THE TIME-LIFE GARDENER'S GUIDE
TIME FRAME
FIX IT YOURSELF
FITNESS, HEALTH & NUTRITION
SUCCESSFUL PARENTING
HEALTHY HOME COOKING
UNDERSTANDING COMPUTERS
LIBRARY OF NATIONS
THE ENCHANTED WORLD
THE KODAK LIBRARY OF CREATIVE PHOTOGRAPHY
GREAT MEALS IN MINUTES
THE CIVIL WAR
PLANET EARTH
COLLECTOR'S LIBRARY OF THE CIVIL WAR
THE EPIC OF FLIGHT
THE GOOD COOK
WORLD WAR II
HOME REPAIR AND IMPROVEMENT
THE OLD WEST

*For information on and a full description of any of the Time-
Life Books series listed above, please call 1-800-621-7026 or
write:*
Reader Information
Time-Life Customer Service
P.O. Box C-32068
Richmond, Virginia 23261-2068

This volume is one of a series that examines the history
and nature of seemingly paranormal phenomena. Other
books in the series include: